WE MOVE
IN NEW DIRECTIONS

Books by H. A. Overstreet

WE MOVE IN NEW DIRECTIONS

INFLUENCING HUMAN BEHAVIOR

THE ENDURING QUEST

ABOUT OURSELVES

We Move in New Directions

BY H. A. OVERSTREET

PROFESSOR AND HEAD
OF THE DEPARTMENT OF PHILOSOPHY AND PSYCHOLOGY
COLLEGE OF THE CITY OF NEW YORK

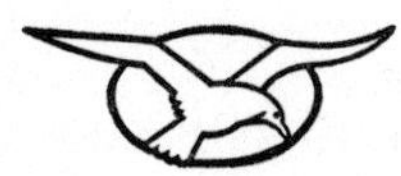

W · W · NORTON & COMPANY, INC.

PUBLISHERS, NEW YORK

PRINTED IN THE UNITED STATES OF AMERICA
FOR THE PUBLISHERS BY THE VAIL-BALLOU PRESS
TYPOGRAPHY BY ROBERT JOSEPHY

CONTENTS

FOREWORD

"THERE'S a hard wind blowing today—which helps, if you're going in the right direction." So a farmer-friend writes me out of the West. The sentence might well express what is happening in our contemporary life. There is a hard wind of new ideas blowing. It started out of somewhere a few decades ago, innocently enough. Now it has risen to a veritable tornado—of new demands, attitudes and valuations—and blessed be we if we are going in the right direction.

For there are winds of ideas as truly as there are winds out of the physical heavens. There come times in the history of life when, with changing conditions, old conceptions suddenly reveal themselves as inadequate or misdirected or actually destructive of life-values, and when fresh ideas blow in to take their place. In such periods new civilizations are born. There is a lustiness and gustiness about life. Out go the accumulated fogs and misconceptions, and the path of life is swept clean for a new going.

The coming to birth of a civilization is by far the most significant event that is occurring today. It is so significant, indeed, that to keep up the prevalent habit of irony or bitterness as to the futilities of our masters and governors seems a waste of precious energy. If a civilization is in process of being born, the most interesting thing to do is to put oneself in line with the kind of thinking that is heading toward the future.

For civilizations, always, are *ideas* or *ways of thinking.* They are ideas that have worked themselves out into objective forms. Thus, mediaeval civilization was the idea of other-worldliness shaped into the stone of cloister and cathedral. Feudal civilization was the idea of the lordship of the highborn expressed in manor and vassal's hut. Capitalistic civilization has been the idea of free enterprise and profit-making built into factory, bank, tariff, army, and navy.

Ideas, in brief, have a way of projecting themselves into concreteness. Indeed, all human history is simply the record of ways of thinking and feeling that have transformed themselves into institutions and behaviors. For an idea, however simple it may be, is always a plan of possible action, and every idea, once consciously held and deeply felt, tends to carry itself out into the action or form indicated.

What are the reconstructive ideas that move, more or less vaguely, in our consciousness today? If one can become aware of them, one may, to an extent, know the direction that our life is taking, and may anticipate how our today is already pushing forward into its tomorrow.

Some people ask apprehensively: "Is there going to be a revolution?" The simple answer is that we are at the present moment passing through three revolutions: an economic, a cultural, and a spiritual. These, singly and together, are of such profound moment that we may readily expect an order of life greatly different from that to which we have grown accustomed.

It is a mistake, of course, to assume that revolutions must be violent. In essence, a revolution simply means a fairly swift and radical change in life-conditions. Whenever such a change takes place, old habits must perforce be altered. Since, however, habit-patterns tend by their very nature to become fixed, every considerable change in conditions meets with a certain amount of resistance. Some individuals are bewildered, others are annoyed, others aroused to a stubborn defensiveness. Whether a revolution turns into violence or not depends altogether upon the readiness with which inevitable changes are met with hospitable intelligence.

There are signs that such intelligence is awakening among us. With an almost uncanny swiftness, the customary willingness to put up with things, which has hitherto characterized our "cultural lag," has in large measure disappeared. Our minds are alive to something momentous that is coming to pass. We are, in short, in a condition of readiness for the new. If, now, we can advance to the next stage of broad and tolerant consideration of how that "new" is to be made into a "better," we may perhaps avoid the tragic consequences that occur whenever stubbornness and ignorance insist upon perpetuating what life, in its onward movements, refuses any longer to tolerate.

This volume is the outgrowth of a course given to adults at The New School for Social Research, in New York City, in the fall of 1932. Again, as in previous years, I wish to thank the members of my class for many an idea that flashed into being in the process of discussion, and for many a critical suggestion that opened up new possibilities. I wish also to thank the editors of *The Forum*, *The Journal of Philosophy*, and *World Unity* for permission to reprint in revised form certain selections from my past writings that have a bearing upon present conditions. The reprinted material is found in *The Forum*, Vol. LIV, No. 1, under the title, *The Government of To-morrow*; in *The Journal of Philosophy*, in Vol. X, No. 5, under the title, *Philosophy and Our Legal Situation*, and in Vol. XII, No. 11, under the title, *Conventional Economics and a Human Valuation*; and in *World Unity*, Vol. VII, No. 4, under the title, *Education and World Culture*.

PART I

TOWARD ECONOMIC SELF-RESPECT

"There's a squeezed world that elbows for attention."
EDWIN ARLINGTON ROBINSON—*Merlin*

CHAPTER 1. THE TRADITIONAL SYSTEM IN ITS PASSING

THE profit-economy is fated to pass away. This now seems certain—for three major reasons. In the first place, the basic motivation involved is too low for what we have come to expect of civilized life. In the second place, the system is too wasteful to recommend itself to an intelligence grown accustomed to the precisions and economies of science. In the third place, it is inherently self-contradictory.

These three reasons, to alert minds, are now so evident that it would seem a waste of time to elaborate. Let us, in a few pages, describe the situation and pass on to what is increasingly occupying our minds: to wit, the type of life-enterprise which is to be the successor of the traditional profit-economy.

MOTIVATION

As to motivation. The profit-economy is a system which has glorified self-interest as the mainspring of life's endeavor. If each man will work for his own interests, declared Adam Smith, an overruling Providence will harmonize the divergencies. Actuated by this spirit of self-interest, men have bestirred themselves, and, with remarkable success, have brought forth the products of their hands and brains. For this reason, the self-interest philosophy has, to many people, seemed justified. But today we begin to realize that man cannot be justified of his products alone; he must be justified of himself. And when we examine what a self-interest philosophy has made of the spirit of man, we are not altogether happy. We behold individuals energetic and resourceful—incredibly so. But on the other hand, we see them occupied chiefly with their financial welfare, utilizing, for their own purposes, the lives of others—beneficently if possible, ruthlessly if necessary; and disregarding the lives of others if they are not essential to the building up of their wealth. We find, in brief, a spirit narrow, aggressive, frequently pitiless, and at all times having only the most tenuous connection with the common welfare.

It can hardly be said, in brief, that the spiritual products of the profit-economy have been an outstanding success. Even when we grant it success as an energy-arouser, we are compelled to confess to its relative failure as a cultivator of spiritual qualities. We are made the more uneasy, since, in our Christian civilization, the profit-economy has compelled us to live within two conflicting systems of motivation. Our religious culture has stressed a love that goes beyond self; our economic culture has stressed a love confined to self. We experience increasing difficulty in reconciling these two, and we begin to suspect that many of our troubles arise out of the fact that self-interest can no longer serve as the chief motivating force even of economic life.

The profit-economy, in short, is passing away because it is not great enough for what is great in us.

WASTE

Secondly, as to waste. We now recognize, with considerable alarm, that self-interests, independent of one another, each going its own way, and all more or less in conflict with one another, lead inevitably to a kind of economic chaos. The *débâcle* of recent years makes us realize that Adam Smith's overruling Providence has been conspicuous by its absence. Indeed, many economists now feel that this overruling Providence must be found within ourselves. They suggest the need for a man-made Supervising Power. Recalling to us the uncontrolled nature of the processes of investment, recalling a production-supply unbalanced by consumption-demand, recalling the over-stimulation of certain enterprises and the under-stimulation of others—indeed, recalling a score and more of confusions that have resulted from free enterprise—they suggest the necessity of something in the nature of a Planning Board. The function of this Planning Board, apparently, is to be that of bringing to pass the harmonization supposed to have been achieved by Adam Smith's beneficent Providence.

But a planned economy will be far from the kind of free enterprise assumed in the profit-system. In the first place, it will cease to give free scope to individual initiative. It will halt the individual in his rugged wish to go his own way and will require that he correlate his enterprises with those of others. In the second place, it will definitively subordinate the hitherto supreme right of individual profit-making to the prior right of the common welfare.

There can be little doubt that we shall go in such a direction as will introduce order into our relative economic chaos. We are weary of the wastes of our system. Nor are we content to be told that Nature herself is wasteful, scattering a thousand seeds that one may come to growth. We retort that man is neither a milkweed nor a spawning fish and that it is time the organizing powers inherent in his rational self be put into action. We ask, in short, that for the confusion of an irresponsible competitiveness there be substituted the orderliness of some kind of responsible coöperation.

THE SELF-CONTRADICTIONS OF THE SYSTEM

Thirdly, as to the self-contradictions inherent in the profit-economy. It is only slowly dawning upon us that we have passed through a second industrial revolution. Those of us who studied our economics in the colleges learned about the industrial revolution that took place in the latter part of the eighteenth and the beginning of the nineteenth centuries. We were taught that, by the introduction of the steam engine, an old order of life passed away and a new was ushered into being. The economics we studied occupied itself wholly with what had happened since that historic event. We were given no inkling of the fact that another historic event had occurred. Perhaps it was too recent to be recognized in its full implication. But in these stirring days, we are beginning to learn that, almost without our knowing it, we have passed through another revolution. Economists are now calling it "The New Industrial Revolution," or, more aptly still, "The Technological Revolution." Feudalism, as we know, passed away when the crude mechanism called the steam engine was made available for human use. That this almost laughably awkward machine should have overturned an order of life which had lasted for centuries seems now almost incredible. The question suggests itself: What will happen as the result of the invention and use of machines far greater in power and efficiency? For within the last few decades, powerful mechanisms have superseded their crude prototypes. Machines are now gas- and electrically-driven, and their output has been so augmented that there is no comparison between them and the simple machines that overthrew feudalism and inaugurated the industrial era. A veritable mechanical revolution has taken place. Unless we recognize this fact, we fail altogether to realize wherein lies one of the essential crises of our times.

When a machine is invented which increases output a thousand-fold, it means that the need for man-power, in that case, is reduced. This is the story of our technological revolution. With a swiftness that has been staggering, machinery has increasingly diminished the need for man-power until, today, it may be said that the more we produce the less we require of human labor.

There is, indeed, the comforting reminder that with the multiplication, diversification, and cheapening of products, new buying has been stimulated; also, that many new occupations have been created. So incredibly rapid, however, has been the growth of productive power through the ingenuity of invention, that productivity has tended constantly to outstrip man-power, with the result that we suffer increasingly from what has been called "technological unemployment."

There are hopeful individuals who believe that when the economic sun begins to rise again and prosperity is once more on the up-curve, those who are now unemployed will find their way back to their positions. This happy anticipation, however, is given its dash of cold water by the economic statisticians. As Mr. George Soule has pointed out in a recent article [1]—and his statement is in line with much prevalent economic thinking—inventions and economies have taken place at so swift a pace that when the upturn comes, there will be need for only a portion of the men formerly employed in the productive industries.

So we come to the first of the self-contradictions inherent in our economic system. It is one which did not manifest itself in the initial stages of the early industrial revolution because of the low productive power of the machines available and the vastness of the hitherto untapped purchasing power. But now that the technological revolution is well under way, the contradiction is so evident as to arouse grave apprehension. It resides in this: *the more the system employs its brain-power in improving its equipment, the more it dis-employs its man-power.* It is a contradiction because the obvious objective of a profit-economy is to supply work, since, if it is to have purchasers for its output, it must have workers who can earn in order to purchase. By displacing

[1] *After Revival—What?* Harper's Magazine, December, 1932.

workers, it displaces its own sources of revenue and so prepares for its own destruction.

Hence the curious dilemma: the higher the productivity of the system, the greater the displacement of man-power, and, by reason of technological unemployment, the lower the buying capacity. Two evils result, then: first, an increasing, and increasingly incurable amount of unemployment; secondly, an increasing, and increasingly incurable diminution of buying power. And the outcome: poverty in the midst of abundance, a production process with the power to produce but without the power to obtain a market for what it produces.

WHEN A GOOD PHILOSOPHY BECOMES EVIL

There is a second contradiction of even graver import. For generations we have been educated in a philosophy of thrift. To save against the lean years, to put by for a rainy day, to accumulate for one's old age, all of these have seemed in the past to be the height of wisdom. "Spendthrift" is still a word of condemnation. The wise man, we have been taught to believe, is he who spends less than he earns and who puts aside a surplus.

In the older generations, when a simpler economy was in effect, this philosophy of thrift worked altogether for human welfare. Man learned his first lessons in the reasonable control of life when, in the abundant days of summer, he stored away food against the time of winter. Doubtless it took him many centuries to learn this simple art of making provision against the future. So deeply imbedded in us has this wisdom of the ages become that we still go on unquestioningly putting by our surpluses.

But a curious thing has happened. A hundred years ago, savings were eventually available for consumption. That was what they were for. Prior to the invention of banks, surplus moneys were stowed away in secret places and brought out when occasion demanded. Later, when banks were instituted, these moneys were placed at the disposal of banks and, by them, were loaned out to inaugurate and to support productive enterprises. For this excellent service, interest was paid. Later, when bonds were issued, surpluses were invested in such securities. Again, as a reward for this service to productive enterprise, interest was given. When common stock was invented, the saver, through investment, became an actual partner in productive enterprises, accepting his share of the profits or the losses.

It all seemed a natural evolution, and in these more recent years we have, without serious questioning of the social consequences, developed the habit of transforming our savings into one or another of the above kinds of investment. But now, suddenly, we begin to be aware of the fact that our quite virtuous behavior has had disastrous consequences for society and for ourselves. To realize these consequences is to be aware of a puzzling dilemma in which we find ourselves. Society makes no adequate provision for taking care of us when we are old or unemployed, or when we are confronted by the various mischances of life. It is therefore still necessary for us to lay up treasures against possible need. In order to save, however, we must invest. There is no other way now open to us. To place our surplus moneys in a stocking and hide them somewhere in a modern home is to be under the constant apprehension of theft or fire. But when we do invest, what happens? As we have shown, if we place the surplus in a bank, the money is reinvested in enterprises chiefly of a productive nature; if we invest in bonds, it is used for the extension chiefly of such enterprises; if we invest in common stock, our surplus makes us partners in the extension of productive enterprises.

Here, then, is a curious paradox. The vast savings of the past few decades have practically all, by very necessity, gone to the building of industrial equipment. As a result, productive industry has become over-expanded. Goods have therefore been poured out upon the market in unprecedented quantities. Meanwhile, we who, in the innocence of our virtue, saved our moneys by thus investing them, were estopped from spending these moneys for consumption purposes. While investment went on at accelerated pace and equipment was expanded into further equipment, we, by the very zeal of our thrift, were lessened in our purchasing power. We were, indeed, like a land-poor folk. With our surpluses tied up, it was impossible for us to buy the very goods our investments produced. Our virtue, therefore, increasingly turned out to be a vice, for the enterprises that our moneys had built were unable to carry on their processes for the reason that we, their potential customers, were too poor to be customers.

Then came the inevitable collapse. The house of business that our moneys had built fell like a house of cards; and with its fall went our savings.

And so we confront the contradiction: the more we save, the more we tend to destroy our savings. Were there a way of saving that would increase consumption-power, the contradiction would instantly disappear. But in our contemporary system, there is practically no such way. Whether we wish it or not, investment means, for the most part, placing our moneys at the service of production-expansion and taking them away from buying power, with the result that, in the end, our savings become as valueless to us as dried leaves in a forest.

Let us repeat that this self-contradiction operates wholly in a system of high technological efficiency. Where machines are of low efficiency, so that goods can be produced only in small quantities, savings can have no such effect as they have in a system where machines have the high productive power that our modern mechanisms possess. The self-contradiction, therefore, is one that has appeared since the afore-mentioned technological revolution. This more recent revolution has made it impossible any longer for the old thrift philosophy to operate unchecked.

What must be the outcome? Must we cease putting by our surpluses and become a civilization of rapid spenders? This is one suggestion which one hears in many quarters. Or shall we change our contemporary system so that saving may still continue but be prevented from operating in such a manner as to destroy itself?

If one may venture a guess, we shall be slow to give up that art of making provision for the future which differentiates us so sharply from most animal life. Instead of proceeding to become lavish and irresponsible spenders, we shall probably set about examining our economic processes in order to discover how provision for the future may be made without, at the same time, destroying that provision itself.

THE TASK AHEAD

In the foregoing, we have discussed three reasons why the profit-economy would seem to be in its decline. In the first place, we noted that its motivation is too low. Whatever the system may be into which we pass, we shall ask that it substitute socialized for unsocialized motivation. Or, perhaps more accurately, we shall demand that it at least give greater opportunity for such socialized motivation. The present system practically compels all of us to be self-seekers. The individual with wide social sympathies has only a precarious place in the system. In all probability, in the relentless competition of self-interests, he fails. The profit-economy, in short, compels us all to live on a level lower than that on which most of us would wish to live; and since, in any event, we must live, we are forced to make our compromise with the system.

In the second place, we noted that the system is highly wasteful. In the building of our machines, we have learned the art of so correlating the mechanical forces at our command as immeasurably to increase our power. We look askance upon a system which makes no thoroughgoing effort to correlate the powers exercised by human beings in the pursuit of the goods of life. We see no reason why such powers should not be rationally organized. We know ourselves to be possessed of logical minds, and we ask increasingly that for the illogical chaos of our traditional economic processes there be substituted logical order.

Finally, we have noted self-contradictions that are inherent in the contemporary system. That the very improvement of our machinery—a magnificent kind of achievement—should degrade man into unemployment and poverty is a puzzling enough outcome. But that the very effort on our part to be wisely anticipatory of the future should make that future all the more precarious is still more puzzling.

Whatever the new system is to be, these puzzles must be resolved. We can no longer proceed happily with a system that destroys its own offspring.

CHAPTER 2. TOOLS AT OUR COMMAND

IF a cabinet-maker is to build an exquisite piece of furniture, he must have tools adequate for the task. Given a stone hammer and a flint chisel, he will not be able to proceed very far. The same is true of a society. If it is to build itself into an order of life ruled by intelligence and a feeling for decent human values, it must have the requisite means. Given warships, jealous nations, self-interested corporations, a fluctuating currency, an antiquated political system, and schools that move in outworn patterns, it will find itself inadequate to the task ahead of it.

Has our present society the tools? It would seem possible to say that there are at least three tools ready at our command today. We have already used them with some measure of success. The difficulty has been that hitherto the tools themselves have been greater than our power to utilize them. If a lad is given a slide-rule, he will have a lovely time making such measurements as he can, but the intricate uses of the rule will be beyond his immature mind. It has been so with these great social tools that we have thus far only partly put into use. In the adolescent heyday of our profit-making economy, we have been unable to grasp their more wide-reaching possibilities. But we are rapidly growing into a kind of social maturity, and there is every reason to believe that we shall, in no very long time, recognize the wider and more genuine applicability of these tools.

INSURANCE

The first of these tools is familiar to us by name, but its philosophical implications and wider social uses are surprisingly unfamiliar. Indeed, we frequently regard insurance as a necessary evil, pay our premiums with a kind of resentment, and almost wish for the fire or the accident that will repay us the moneys we have invested. But when we examine the matter carefully, we realize that in insurance man has achieved a truly remarkable invention. Like the steam engine, it was conceived a good many centuries ago, but it has been wrought into a major instrumentality only within recent decades. Thus, in the days of Rome, there existed associations of artisans which paid the surviving dependents of their members a funeral sum in return for an initiation fee and monthly premiums. In mediaeval times there were associations which provided funds for freeing comrades from imprisonment, or from losses due to fire, or for the death of cattle, or for replacing cattle stolen from members of the guild.

Here was recognition of the fact that by the pooling of small contributions, effective aid could be rendered to an individual in case of disaster. But such recognition needed a stronger impetus to become widespread. It was given by the great expansion of Italy's maritime trade about the middle of the fourteenth century. Insurance now became important enough to be made into a business enterprise. Stock companies were formed in the eighteenth and nineteenth centuries. Two marine insurance companies were founded in England in 1720, while in Germany the first corporation for marine insurance was founded in Hamburg in 1765.

Life insurance in its present form did not arise until almost a hundred years later than the modern type of marine and fire insurance. There were reasons for this. Life insurance, to be safe, requires careful statistical mortality estimates, and these have only recently been available. Also, there was prevalent in the earlier centuries the feeling that to insure one's life was to engage in a kind of gamble with God. Hence, for this reason, and because of the possible criminal excesses which it might entail, life insurance was actually forbidden.

With the increase of productive enterprise in the nineteenth century, the need for some such mutually protective device became increasingly apparent. "The highly differentiated economic life of the second half of the nineteenth century brought with it numerous cultural gains accompanied by new dangers and new requirements: the growth of railroads; the increase in factory production and the liability of the entrepreneur; improved methods of building, especially the wider use of glass windowpanes, the installation of water pipes in dwelling houses; the extension of credit and mortgages; the rise of the automobile and of aircraft. All these innovations made room for the spread of the idea of insurance. Accident insurance was introduced in 1845 and liability insurance in 1876; these were followed by glass insurance, insurance against damage to water pipes and so on. Corporate fidelity bonding was first practiced in 1840, title insurance and credit insurance developed in the 1890's, workmen's compensation met the need of statutory requirements of the early twentieth century, and public liability insurance, especially of automobile risks, has expanded rapidly in the last decade." [1]

BRINGING A SPIRITUAL IDEAL TO EARTH

Thus we note the gradually increasing use of this social tool. There are no indications that the tool is basically defective and that it is eventually to be superseded. On the contrary, all indications point to its further development. We discover, in fact, that "the World War did not exert as destructive an effect upon the position of insurance in economic life as might have been supposed, and between 1918 and 1923 more new companies were founded than in any previous five-year period." [2]

We are accustomed to think of insurance as wholly an economic enterprise, for when we take out insurance for ourselves it is usually at the solicitation of someone interested in selling it to us. We do not, for the most part, discover our spiritual leaders admonishing us to adopt the ways of insurance. This, doubtless, is one of the many indications of the inability of most leaders of this type to translate spiritual insights into practical life. Their spiritual

[1] Alfred Manes, *Encyclopedia of the Social Sciences,* Vol. VIII, page 98. By permission of The Macmillan Company.

[2] *Ibid.,* page 98.

admonitions all too frequently are hung aloft in a vague cloudland of unattainable aspirations. But only the slightest thought must convince us that insurance is in reality a spiritual idea put into practice. It is, in short, one important application of the idea: "Bear ye one another's burdens."

If one sees this, it becomes clear that in inventing insurance, man discovered one way in which individual life might be lived with effective mutuality. The premium which the individual pays serves not only to protect him. It also protects others. And the premiums which they pay protect not only them but him. Each, in this case, is for all and all are for each. Social-minded individuals have a way, at times, of pleading for the latter principle as one to be realized in the future, not understanding that in insurance it already operates with an effectiveness that witnesses to its validity.

Thus we have a tool already at hand in which we can have confidence. Hitherto its uses have been chiefly motivated by personal interests. As we become aware of its wider possibilities, however, we shall doubtless increasingly recognize it as one most effective tool for achieving social justice. For we are more and more aware that the growing complication of life makes it impossible for each individual to bear his burdens alone. Many of the difficulties he confronts are not of his own creation. The illnesses which he contracts because of occupational stresses and strains in an industrialized society are not to be attributed to his own neglect, but to forces against which he is powerless to protect himself. The unemployment which suddenly comes upon him out of the blue is not of his own making, but is due to economic displacements which he is helpless to control. His poverty in old age may not be due to thriftlessness or sloth, for in a world of economic insecurity even the best of us may, in the end, meet financial disaster.

It is impossible any longer, therefore, to repeat the complacent platitude of individualism which required that a man ruggedly take care of his own ills. Where the ills are socially created, they must be socially borne. Insurance can be a kind of instrument of social justice, giving to each man his due in return for his participation in society's mutual enterprise.

PUBLIC WEALTH

There is a second social tool at our command. It, also, has a history of long use, but in recent generations we have been suspicious of it, as if it might do us some irreparable harm. The reason for this is not difficult to discover. Following both the industrial revolution and the revolution in thought brought about by the Darwinian hypothesis, we became convinced that if an individual was to possess the goods of life, he must win them by his individual enterprise. To give him anything freely was to go counter to the philosophy of rigorous competition and survival of the fittest. That seemed, in the nineteenth century, to be the last word in wisdom. To give free access to the goods of life was supposed to pauperize individuals and to weaken their fibre. "To each according to what he can earn for himself," was the strict maxim of nineteenth century individualism.

Older centuries viewed the matter differently. Then, in many cases, it was taken for granted that a community was civilized in proportion to the public wealth which it could place at the disposal of its citizens. In Athens, for example, there were the temples, the gymnasium, and the public theatre; in Rome, the marbles of the Forum, the amphitheatre, and the public baths; in mediaeval ages, the great cathedrals.

In the nineteenth century we seemed to plunge into a new kind of barbarism, the barbarism of what Delisle Burns has called "public indigence and private wealth." [3] The major energies of men were devoted to private fortune-making. Public wealth was both neglected and decried. It should be no surprise to us that this new barbarism bred the uglinesses of our industrial cities and countrysides. Where life was almost wholly a private, self-interested affair, little attention could be paid to that which concerned no single individual but only all individuals taken together.

We have come limping out of that recent plunge into barbarism. Much of its unloveliness still clings to us—cities that are monstrosities of huddled planlessness; poverty within a stone's throw of riches; high-pressure salesmanship and low-pressure citizenship; education turning out bigger and better go-getters.

Perhaps no more poignant example of the carry-over of that barbarism of private wealth-getting could be found than on the river's side of the "wealthiest" city in the world. There, where streams of motor cars incessantly pass,

[3] Delisle Burns, *Leisure,* page 12 (Century Company).

and where the mansions of the rich and the skyscrapers of financial enterprise overlook the Hudson, a crowd of non-descript shacks shelters—if that word may be used—a ragged army of those who have been unfortunate enough to meet the full impact of an economic calamity beyond their control. In their huts of tin and rotten boards they shiver through the winter while thousands of nearby apartments are empty of occupants. No one is brazen enough to suggest that these, through some public arrangement, should be used for the housing of the shelterless. These apartments represent private wealth.

Within a few blocks of this scene, one beholds children trooping to school. Most of them, obviously, are children of the poor. In many cases, indeed, there are evident signs of under-nourishment. But no official stops them at the school door to enquire whether they have sufficient money to pay for their schooling. Were such an official suddenly to confront these children and turn back all save those who could pay, we should cry out in astonishment: "This is barbarism." We feel gratified at the sight of the children entering freely into educational opportunities and we regard ourselves as civilized to the extent that we grant access to this essential life-need.

A few blocks further on we come to a park. Individuals pass in and out with complete freedom. Again, we are gratified at this, for we find ourselves in no mood to begrudge the open spaces of lawns and trees even to those whose circumstances are obviously of the meagerest. Again, a little further on, we come to a museum that houses priceless treasures. The doors are open, and all manner of people are entering and leaving.

We need not carry on the tale. When we remember our public schools and colleges, parks and playgrounds, galleries, museums, and public libraries, we are proud that our communities possess these treasures. We realize that they are in large degree the measure of our civilization and that if they were swept away and a return were made to a régime of exclusive private wealth, we should have turned our civilization back toward barbarism.

USING THIS TOOL

Athens used the tool of public wealth to build up a memorable civilization. We ourselves, despite the powerful pressure toward private fortune-making, have used it—in school, park, museum, library, roadway—to mitigate the harshness of an economy in which each is permitted to possess only what he can purchase through his earnings. Where there is public wealth, the rule of "to each according to his earnings" is abrogated, for no individual could possibly earn enough to give himself the riches that lie in public library, park, museum, school, and college. But each individual needs what lies in these. Hence every civilization which opens its treasures of public wealth to its citizens operates on another principle: "to each according to his needs."

Here, then, is an instrumentality—public wealth—which has had its long history and which, in the course of that history, has proved its effectiveness. If we are to move forward, it will not be by diminishing the scope of this instrumentality but rather by expanding it in ways not yet contemplated. We shall doubtless ere long come to take even more seriously this principle of "to each according to his needs." We shall not be content merely to respond to the essential needs of the mind and refuse to respond to the essential needs of the body. Particularly we shall refuse to do this as we realize that poverty, in these days of high-geared industry and finance, is, for the most part, due to no reprehensible behavior on the part of those who are deprived of the major necessities of life. As we become conscious of the fact that, in our society, work and earning are mainly outside the control of individuals and that unemployment and financial destitution come to the good and the evil alike, we shall see no pauperizing effect, but only strict justice, in the granting of as free access to food, shelter, clothing, transportation, and medical care as now obtains in the case of books, pictures, parks, and education. In short, it is not unlikely that before very long we shall take this well-tried instrumentality of public wealth and expand it until it covers all the really essential needs of man.

COMMANDING OUR RESOURCES

There is a third tool at our command. It is one only recently shaped to our uses. As in the case of the other two tools—insurance and public wealth—it has scarcely as yet been utilized save in restricted ways. It has possibilities that may make it as effective as these other two in helping to transform life into something more satisfyingly civilized.

We refer to a graduated income tax. Doubtless this tool has not yet come into fuller use because the principle underlying it has not been generally grasped. Graduated income tax is regarded rather in the light of a punishment. Those who possess great wealth seem to look upon it thus, resentfully. Those who do not possess great wealth regard it with glee. In neither case is the genuine nature of the tax understood.

A graduated income tax is the recognition on the part of a society that those who participate in its processes should not only receive its benefits in accordance with their needs but should contribute to those benefits in proportion to their capacity. It is obvious that no individual accumulates income by his sole individual energy and alertness. What comes to him comes in large measure because of all kinds of social advantages—the scientific and cultural status of his day, inventions, books, newspapers, population-growth. His power to tap these resources increases rapidly with his increase of income, so that the man of twenty thousand dollars in income, let us say, has an access to social resources many more than twenty times that of a man who has an income of a thousand dollars. While in arithmetic two hundred dollars plus two hundred dollars equals four hundred dollars, in economic enterprise two hundred dollars plus two hundred dollars equals five or six or more hundreds of dollars. There is, in short, in this case and in cases like it, an increase that is more in the nature of a geometrical than an arithmetical progression. It is fair, then, that the wealthier individual should give back to his society in proportion to the increased power of his appropriation.

But why give back? There is no answer to this on the basis of traditional individualistic economy. In that economy, each man is accountable only to himself, and he is to be congratulated upon all that he can procure and hold for himself. It is this individualistic principle, however, which is now being increasingly discredited. It lacks the element of good sportsmanship that one expects of a decently social-minded being. We now recognize that social life is a process requiring the most generous give-and-take; and we expect, therefore, that he who participates in its processes, receiving of its benefits, should, in the spirit of fair sportsmanship, give in just proportion to what he receives.

PREVENTING OVER-INVESTMENT

One of the chief problems ahead of us, as we have shown in the previous chapter, is to divert moneys from over-investment. This cannot satisfactorily be done by old-fashioned hoarding, since hoarding, by withdrawing currency from circulation, would involve us in even greater evils. The real problem is not to withdraw moneys, but to contrive to have them so used that consumption- rather than production-goods are increased.

Consider a person with an income of one thousand dollars. All of his income will be used for consumption purposes. Every dollar that he spends keeps the wheels of industry turning and the marts of commerce at work. Consider now a person with an income of a hundred thousand dollars. In all probability, not the whole of that amount will be used for consumption purposes. Much of it will be laid aside and invested. As we mount the scale of income, we find that more and more is laid aside as unnecessary for consumption purposes and that what is thus laid aside is, through investment, injected into productive industry.

The higher the incomes, in short, the greater the volume of investment. To restate this in the terms above suggested: the higher the incomes, the more dangerous the effect upon the common welfare.[4]

The problem of the future is obviously that of utilizing higher surpluses so as to make them not dangerous but beneficial. Apparently the only way to do this is, as they grow larger, to divert them in increasing proportion into the production of consumption-goods.

To this end, we have this tool of a graduated income tax. To divert moneys to social uses through taxation means taking them out of the production field. It means using them for roads, parks, schools, colleges, hospitals, museums, libraries. All of these are consumption-goods. No one of them is an equipment for adding to production. The more moneys, therefore, we are able to turn into the creation of such consumption-goods, the more we take away from the over-expansion of production-processes.

Two results, then, would be accomplished by a more extended and effective use of a graduated income tax. In the first place, to the degree that we increased taxation in the

[4] A searching presentation of this point is made by David Cushman Coyle in *The Irrepressible Conflict* (David Cushman Coyle, New York City).

higher brackets, we should halt the hitherto uncontrolled processes of pouring moneys into over-equipment. In the second place, we should augment the funds available for public wealth.

Here, then, is one fairly clear way ahead. It is a way that does not require the scrapping of our traditional system entire. It requires merely that we make a wise diversion of surplus funds into consumption-uses. It is a way that is relatively easy to take, for we have already begun to learn how to use this tool. That there are grave obstacles goes without saying. Those who now are the masters of our life—the owners of large resources of capital—are not likely to surrender their privileges without struggle. But the most powerful agency in the world is a valid idea. There was never a time in modern history when a valid idea was more widely sought. As long as we have no clear thought, our protests are but bewildered cries for relief. Once, however, we grasp an idea that points the way ahead, a public opinion can develop which will in good time be strong enough to overcome the opposition of privileged interests. A steeply graduated income tax is undoubtedly one of the means whereby an effective balance of production and consumption is to be achieved through the diversion of surplus funds into forms of public wealth.

CONCLUSION

Three tools, then, for the shaping of our future society—two of them of well-worn usage, the third of recent invention. Each of these is not only a tool for social use, but is expressive of a genuine principle of social life. In insurance, we find expressed the principle of a social bearing of burdens; in public wealth, the principle "to each according to his needs"; in graduated income tax, the principle "from each according to his capacity." What is hopeful is that they have already worked, that they are working today, and that they do not, like so many other instrumentalities of our economic life, need to be discarded. Retaining them, but extending their uses, we may have it within our power, through them, to bring about not a little of the needed transformation of our society.

CHAPTER 3. A SHORT VIEW AND A LONG

THE development of public wealth has not, during our century of individualism, been achieved without a struggle. Practically every effort to open resources freely to all individuals, whatever their pecuniary status, has been met by the cry, "Pauperization!" Thus the proposal, urged in America first of all by organizations of workers, to establish public education, roused the privileged classes to resentment. Public education, they held, would not only pauperize the masses by taking away from them the incentive to earn the means for schooling; it would work a grievous injustice to those who must bear the heavy burden of taxation in behalf of children not their own.

However, the fight for public education was won; and it would be a curiously anti-social individual who would today wish public education out of existence. Nevertheless, every effort to extend such education beyond the elementary grades had to be bitterly fought. But step by step, we have advanced until we are, in large measure, a society which opens freely to everyone the opportunity for an education from the elementary to the higher levels.

Public libraries are an institution of fairly recent origin. A hundred years ago there were none. If an individual was wealthy enough to own books, he was to that degree fortunate; if he was poor, he simply had to do without. The history of the long effort to domesticate the idea of public libraries is instructive as an instance of the social resistance to a new idea and also of the triumphant quality which lies in an idea of genuine social worth. The idea did win; and only a peculiarly obtuse individual would feel that it has not brought something of very great worth to our civilization.

The same tale could be repeated in the case of many another advance beyond private to public wealth. Public museums, art galleries, parks, hospitals, clinics—all these were virtually unknown to our forefathers. They are now part of the accepted order of life, and we should count it a severe setback to civilization if these forms of public wealth were eliminated.

ARE THERE FURTHER STAGES?

Have we come to the end of this development? Or, with poverty, insecurity, and widespread frustration still in our midst, are there further advances that would seem inevitable?

What, one may ask at this point, is the principle involved in the making public of certain forms of wealth? Obviously it is a fairly simple one. Public schools, for example, were established because education is an indispensable need. Individuals cannot properly carry on their lives under a condition of illiteracy and ignorance. But adequate education is beyond the means of most persons. Hence schools were made public on the principle that where there is an indispensable need which most individuals are incapable of satisfying, it is the obligation of society to meet that need.

Periodically, in our modern life, we face a disturbing situation. Individuals who, in themselves, are quite blameless, find themselves without employment. Naturally they are thereby deprived of the means wherewith to purchase the basic necessities: food, clothing, shelter, medical care, and the transportation which might place them in the way of securing work.

In the economic philosophy of individualism, as we have said, it was assumed that everyone was himself responsible for obtaining these basic necessities. If he could not obtain them, it was taken for granted that he was incompetent or lazy or both. The economic individualist could repeat with the psalmist: "Never yet saw I the righteous forsaken." What we periodically discover is that we have the righteous—the willing and the capable—with us in uncountable numbers, and that they are "forsaken."

We face, then, a situation in which individuals with the best of intentions and with the most strenuous of efforts are not able to obtain the employment by which to earn the necessities of life. Obviously, then, there is but one conclusion to be drawn. Our civilization is at a point where some other principle must be applied. The granting of free access to necessary food, shelter, clothing, medical care, and transportation in time of unemployment becomes now a social obligation.

This will be met with the same old outcry that it is

pauperization. It might be answered that there is no worse pauperization than charity, and that the morale of millions of people is broken by the necessity of begging aid. Nor can the matter be lightly brushed aside by the remark that this, at present, is only a temporary necessity—that, for the most part, all individuals who wish employment can normally find it. This, as we now easily see, is false—for two reasons. In the first place, the profit-economy, because of the necessity for practicing "respectable sabotage" in order to keep up the level of prices, must operate with a continual margin of unemployment. In the second place, technological unemployment promises to increase rather than decrease.

It is essential, therefore, to realize that normal access to the necessities of life is outside the power of a large part of the population, and that, in the present economy, this must always be so. Inability on the part of individuals to secure the very necessities of life is, then, to be set down, not to incompetence or laziness, but to a system which inevitably operates to the hurt of some part of its members.

FROM CHARITY TO A GUARANTEE

We are at a point in our social history, then, at which we must either maintain a recurring—it may now be said, continuing—injustice or advance to a stage in which access to the necessities is by some normal arrangement guaranteed. That this is now being recognized is a sign not only of an awakening social conscience but of a distrust of an economic philosophy which places the burden of subsistence-getting wholly upon the shoulders of individuals who are themselves incapable of controlling the larger fluctuations of finance and industry. We are compelled, in short, to consider ways in which they may be guaranteed at least the decencies of life.

This is an exceedingly important point to have reached in our social history. During all the past centuries "relief" has not been regarded as a social obligation, to be met in an organized way, and particularly in a way that visits no humiliation upon the recipients of the relief. On the contrary, it has been regarded as a kind of emergency assistance given in a spirit of kindliness by the more fortunate members of a society. If, however, the principle above expressed is sound, the time has arrived for incorporating into the social structure a permanent means whereby indispensable needs will be automatically met when the meeting of them by individuals is beyond their power.

What is chiefly necessary for the accomplishment of such an end is a change in our customary point of view. We still, in large measure, are unable to rid ourselves of the age-old notion that a person's food, shelter, clothing, medical care, and transportation should be secured by his own individual efforts. Once, however, we become convinced that there are circumstances under which his own efforts are quite without avail, we shall be prepared to put the social principle above described into operation.

To that end, the tool of insurance at least is at our command. We have already noted how aptly it expresses the spiritual principle: "Bear ye one another's burdens." A decently civilized society will not tolerate a condition in which burdens are imposed that are altogether too heavy for individuals to bear. Insurance against the incidence of worklessness will be made readily possible by that other social tool to which we have referred, a steeply graduated income tax. There will, indeed, be further resources from which an insurance fund can be accumulated, but there is every reason why part of the resources of a graduated tax should be reserved for times of economic disaster.

A kind of strict justice is here involved. For in our society, under the present system, it is the facility for building large fortunes which chiefly brings about the instability of the economic structure. There is justice, then, in diverting to the relief of unemployment a portion of the very fortunes that tend to cause unemployment.

There are many ways in which a plan of unemployment insurance can be devised. We shall not discuss these in detail. The important point at present is to indicate that some such effective type of mutual aid is essential to civilized society. Without doubt, it may be taken for granted that an unemployment insurance fund is to be the next addition to our hitherto organized forms of public wealth.

TOWARD A LONG VIEW

This, however, takes us only a short distance toward the tomorrow of our civilization. Undeserved and unpredictable destitution remains indeed a barbarity in our midst, and swift measures must undoubtedly be taken both to relieve it and to prevent its recurrence. Meanwhile there is another inadequacy in our present-day life which demands attention. Here, again, as is so frequently the case, it is a habit of mind that stands in our way. It will be necessary for us to change this age-long habit if we are to advance to a more acceptable order of civilization.

When Adam ate of the tree of the knowledge of good and evil, the folktale tells us, he was driven from the Garden and condemned to labor by the sweat of his brow. For Adam, thereafter, life was a difficult and precarious process of "making a living." He had little time to raise his eyes from his work. The curse of compulsory labor was on him, and all that he might otherwise have been or wished to be, was now beyond his power. He was "a slave to bed and board."

With a curious finality we have accepted this tale as properly descriptive of man's destiny on earth. To labor all one's days for the sheer necessities of life has seemed to us to be the inevitable—and, on the whole, justifiable—human portion. Throughout history, we have noted indeed with a kind of envy certain individuals apparently released from this necessity: on the one hand, highborn individuals, inheritors of aristocratic privileges; on the other, individuals born with silver spoons in their mouths, inheritors of fortunes. We have envied them, but at the same time we have disapproved of them. Truly virtuous life, we have believed—thus transmuting our misfortune into a blessing—must fulfill its destiny of hard and even distasteful labor. No doubt our feeling that this is the virtuous life has been enhanced by the fact that these fortunate ones were always released at the cost of others from the human destiny of labor. They were, in a sense, parasitic creatures, able to do as they pleased with their lives because others were prohibited from doing likewise.

The history of man has, in the main, been the history of two classes, those condemned to a lifetime of labor, and those released from such lifetime of labor because of a control exercised over the rest of their fellows. This condition of affairs, as we easily realize, still continues in the form of a civilization made up of the masses who work under compulsion for a living and the favored few who, by some fortunate chance, do, both in their work-life and their play-life, very much as they please.

A kind of bitterness has crept into life as this apparent inequity in human arrangements has been contemplated. But because the situation has seemed always to be an incurable one, the working masses have rationalized their toil into a kind of self-justification. They have shaped the view that there is something righteous about work-for-a-living and something unrighteous about living freely in accordance with one's interests.

Indeed, this habit of lauding work-for-a-living as a source of virtue has become so fixed in our social consciousness that we never seem able to conceive even the possibility of a society in which servitude to subsistence-getting is reduced to a minimum and in which all individuals have the right to devote the major energies of their life to that which comports with their powers and interests.

This justifying of our own servitudes would be humorous were it not so pathetic. Here is a fine old gentleman who, for the past twenty years, has locked and unlocked safety-vault boxes for depositors. Before that he was a subaltern accountant. He would like to have worked at his violin; but with marriage and children, it was necessary to earn a living, and the violin had to be put aside for sterner enterprise. The violin has now pretty well faded out of his life, for the shadows of the safety-vault have gathered about his later years, and the early musical enthusiasm has dimmed. If he had been born rich—then it would have been different. He would have traveled, studied with excellent teachers, learned to compose music.

The tale could be repeated a thousandfold. The poet Gray must have been thinking of something like this when he spoke of full many a flower born to blush unseen. He must have meant that the full potentialities of a great many men and women have never yet been released. A kind of rigor of necessity is early imposed upon them. They must do what they must do, not what they wish to do. Thus what they have it in them to be—their *to ti en einai,* as Aristotle would say—is forever being subordinated to the fairly animal enterprise of securing the means of livelihood.

For this is, after all, only a kind of animal enterprise. Man—even the average man—has far more capabilities in him than working for food and shelter. He has capacities for creation, invention, appreciation, exploration. He is potentially poet, dramatist, story-teller, scientist, philosopher, artist. Civilization thus far has permitted these potentialities to come to fruition in him only by accident or good fortune. For the most part, it has made him into "a decent product of life's ironing out." If, indeed, courage and hope manage to survive, after a fashion, in even the most somber of circumstances, such courage and hope must expend themselves for ends no higher than those of merely perpetuating existence:

> *"Behold this marvel now of humankind:*
> *That men, defrauded, still are strong to find*
> *Courage at night to plan ingenious schemes*
> *Of earning meager bread, that there still gleams*
> *Within their minds the promise of success*
> *If they but reach beyond their weariness,*
> *That in the morning hope sufficient soars*
> *To send them knocking on indifferent doors."*[1]

BORN INTO RICHES

"If he had been born rich" . . . Will it seem extravagant if we say that, in our present civilization, being born rich is now within the range of everyone?

It is, in fact, within the range of everyone for the first time in history. All the older societies were poverty-stricken in the sense that their struggles for subsistence were carried on by means of such primitive tools that they could never emerge to the full security of a safe surplus. Agriculture was a primitive art, capable of winning from the soil only a meager portion of its possible yield. And even for this meager winning, much human labor was required. Manufacturing also was a primitive art. To clothe and house themselves and to shape the necessary equipment

[1] Ruth Douglas Keener, *A. D. 1933*, in *The Survey* (Midmonthly), June, 1933. By permission of the author and *The Survey*.

for living required continuous labor on the part of the majority of men and women.

This was the era of deficit, as it has been called. Life was continually on or near the danger line of destitution, and only by the unremitting toil of men, women, and even children could the necessities and a few of the luxuries be wrung from an apparently niggardly Nature. Obviously under such conditions the luxuries were confined to the more powerful few, while even the necessities of these few were supplied by the lifelong work of the many.

This is the pattern of life to which we have grown accustomed. We have been habituated to it so long that any other seems difficult, if not impossible, to conceive. But we have advanced into another era—that of surplus. Through the mechanisms devised during the past few decades, we have gained such a power over the resources of life that we are now able to capture and use these in increasing abundance. We can draw forth a kind of measureless wealth from our world. Thus, as societies, we need not starve, nor go raggedly clothed, nor live shelterless. With an incredible swiftness and variety, the machines we have devised pour riches into our life. We are now all born into a world that is astonishingly wealthy.

Thus the older requirement that the greater number of individuals live meager lives in order that a few should be able to live rich ones, need no longer obtain. A survey of the mechanical powers at our command indicates that a comparatively few hours of work per day on the part of each individual could, if the work were socially organized and utilized, supply not only the basic needs of all of us, but most of the luxury needs as well.

We are born into a rich world—and most of us are poor. This curious contradiction is being so often expressed nowadays that we need not dwell upon it. We may take it for granted that its increasingly vivid realization indicates that the contradiction is on the way to being resolved. For once a conviction is born in our minds, it has a way of working out to its conclusion with a kind of swift inevitability. What we are interested in at this point is to note the implications of this new social wealth. Fundamentally it makes possible the achievement of a new pattern of life for all of us, one so different from that to which we have grown accustomed that most individuals are unable without great difficulty to adjust their minds to its amazing possibilities. It is the pattern of a life freed, for the major portion of its time, from work-for-a-living that is a mere servitude. It is the pattern of a life granted the liberty to do what it fundamentally aspires to do; of a life made free to act in terms of its genuine interests and powers. It is, in short, the pattern of the kind of life we should like to live, but which, by the circumstance of a world confused as to its objectives and awkward in its processes, we have, for the most part, been denied.

USING INDIVIDUALS AS ENDS

There are some of us whose work-for-a-living follows along the lines of our major interests. We are, of course, the fortunate ones. Our work is not primarily for subsistence-needs. These needs, indeed, are fulfilled; but what is more to the point is that *we* are fulfilled. We have the rare privilege of spending a lifetime developing what we have it in us to be.

It should be obvious that a society in which all individuals were given this same privilege would be one far more civilized and fruitful than any as yet realized. For, as we have seen, in all past societies—and in our own—the greater number of individuals have been compelled to forego most of what they may have it in them to be for what they are forced by life-necessities to do.

Kant laid down the moral law that we should treat humanity, whether in ourselves or in others, as an end and not simply as a means. It may be said that all societies thus far developed have compelled most lives to exist solely as means—means to subsistence-getting, or worse still, means to getting subsistence for others.

To treat a life as an end signifies to permit that life to realize its true possibilities. Where such permission is not granted, where the customary order of existence is one which subordinates the individual to ends whose fulfillment negates his possibilities or holds them in abeyance, the society fails to realize its moral purpose. It is a society, therefore, which is still on a sub-moral level. Of such a nature have been all societies up to and including our own.

THE NEW MOVEMENT OF OUR LIFE

We may, however, safely assert that the most obvious movement of life today is toward a genuinely moral society. More than ever we are concerning ourselves with the fulfillment of the individual. We are beginning to make a fair start on it with the child, for increasingly, as wise parents and teachers, we seek not to impose upon him our adult patterns but to elicit his own potentialities. Again, in the treatment of delinquents and criminals, we are rapidly developing an unwillingness to resort to the old methods of punitive suppression. We are beginning to attempt in some effective manner to reconstruct the individual so that he may learn to operate as a true personality. Increasingly, too, a psychological objective begins to prevail among us. We have learned to speak of maladjusted individuals, and we search out the means whereby they may be properly adjusted. Our attitude toward marriage has significantly changed in the direction of granting to individuals the right to find in marriage a genuine happiness. When the marriage conditions go counter to such happiness, we grant the privilege of severing the bonds.

This new conception of life begins also to penetrate even into regions of politics. Old-fashioned politics were simply, and quite unashamedly, power-politics. A state was a force-organization, and it was a successful state if it was strong enough to coerce other states into submission. While the relations of states are still far from admirable, we at least note a movement in a new direction. Thus, to take only a single example, the figure of a Gandhi, recognized and applauded by millions throughout the world, is indicative of the fact that the old days of ruthless suppression of one people by another are very nearly over. The new statecraft bids fair to build itself on the moral principle that each people must be treated as an end in itself and not as a means to the wealth and glory or even the self-assumed world obligations of other peoples.

Finally the new conception begins to permeate vocational life. Young people are increasingly being guided into the kind of work for which they are fitted and which fits them. While the movement of vocational guidance is still in its infancy, and while, for the most part, it is defeated because of the fact that the economic order exists primarily for profit-making and hardly at all for individual fulfillment, the very fact that the movement is growing in extent and in scientific insight indicates that the center of attention is shifting to problems of the well-being of the individual.

THE NEW PATTERN EMERGES

And so the new pattern of life begins to emerge. The old pattern was, as we have seen, chiefly one of life-defeat. Uncounted numbers went to their graves—and still do—without having had the slightest opportunity to live up to the level of their possibilities. For that reason, under the old pattern, life, on the whole, was a poverty-stricken affair—mentally and emotionally. Even when societies became materially rich, the life of most men and women was mentally and emotionally barren. Individuals were condemned to labor at work that did not elicit their valid powers and interests, and while such individuals developed virtues requisite to that servitude, these were in the main the elementary ones of endurance and reliability. They were not the virtues of a true life-release, the kind that could build a world of creativity and high fellowship.

Our world is astonishingly rich in materials, and we now ask that it should be rich also in mental and emotional life. What we begin to ask for, in short, is more than an equality of the vote. We ask as well for an equality of cultural opportunity—in brief, for that equality which assumes in every individual latent interests and powers, and which so organizes social forces that these latencies are given their full chance.

Obviously, however, this new democracy of culture cannot be realized save as the major portion of the life of everyone is in some way rescued from compulsory subsistence-getting that is out of keeping with the individual's essential interests and powers.

Can this be done? The simple answer is: it can probably be done if we are willing to set about doing it. What chiefly stands in the way is no material obstacle—for we have riches aplenty—but a psychological attitude. Old habits of thinking continue to govern us so firmly that we simply do not conceive of an order of existence in which the major energizing of all is in line with their fundamental selfhood.

But ideas, let us repeat, have a way of moving swiftly once they are grasped as true. Our contemporary society has already grasped the first part of the idea: namely, that the individual has a right to the development of his latent powers. When the second part of the idea is grasped —that a life-sentence to work which has no relation to one's self is the chief obstacle which stands in the way of such development—we shall move rapidly out of an old order into a new and far happier one.

There are, then, two problems that confront us—one a short-view problem, the other a long-view one. We must quickly relieve the burden of undeserved and unpreventable worklessness by some means that visits no humiliation upon the recipients of relief. But, in the second place, we must steadily advance toward such an organization of the rich resources of our civilization as will make possible the release of individuals from mere subsistence-getting into the kind of life in which they are able more fully than now to realize what they truly have it in them to be.

CHAPTER 4. FOCUSING ON THE LONG VIEW

WE come, then, to the challenging question: how can this release of life be achieved? Obviously not, it would seem, by the present form of society, in which all major processes are organized to the end of making profit. Factories are built with profit in mind; banks and commercial houses are run with it in view. Cities, in their layout and their rentals, are adapted to profit-making needs. Schools are utilized to prepare oncoming generations for profit-making enterprise. Newspapers are in large measure the media of the profit-makers; books, for the most part, are written and sold for profit; and even the intimacies of the home are invaded by the insistent voice of the advertising profit-seeker.

A civilization bent on making profits can hardly be greatly concerned about making individuals. It is for this reason that practically no attention is paid either to fitting individuals to the kind of work that elicits their powers and interests, or, equally important, to organizing work so that it is fit for individuals. The assumption in a profit-making society is that individuals are made for profit and not profit for individuals. Hence the dark picture of a society of men and women serving the machinery of production and distribution in ways that diminish rather than augment their effective life.

THE NEED OF A NEW MOTIVE

If a true release of life is ever to be achieved, it can only be by a society which ceases to be in paramount degree actuated by the profit-making motive. Another motive will have to be substituted: that of fulfilling human life. A society which adopts this other motive will inevitably reorganize its procedures throughout. Factory processes that cramp and distort the individual will be regarded as abominations quite irrespective of whether they make profits or not. Commercial processes that dull the moral sense, that make life petty and mean, or grasping and aggressive, will, however successful their money-making power, be held to be evil. Such a society, in short, will regard individuals rather than profits as of chief value, and it will organize its processes so that the capacities and interests of individuals shall as far as is humanly possible be developed.

Should such a society ever be achieved, it will undoubtedly operate in two ways. In the first place, it will bend its best scientific efforts toward learning how to discover latent capacities and interests, whereupon it will apply its most careful tests to each individual, so that, as the years of schooling pass, each may become increasingly aware of the area in which his happiest and most effective functioning lies. All education, in short, will be permeated by the idea that its chief objective is to help individuals to find their true areas of functioning—those areas in which they are at once happiest and most fully contributory to the whole enterprise of life.

In the second place, such a society will make every possible effort so to organize the work processes that they shall fit the capacities and interests of individuals. If work is cramping, the best effort will be made to change conditions until it is no longer injurious. If work is monotonous, ways and means will be sought so to introduce variety into the processes as to prevent dulling and stagnation. In brief, such a society will regard the work-processes primarily as means not to profit but to life-fulfillment, and it will severely eliminate, or, if it cannot quite do this, it will ameliorate work conditions that tend to defeat the end of true living.

We have a way of describing our present profit-making system as individualism. As a matter of fact, it is nothing of the kind, for its interest is not in individuals but in the gain that can be made out of them. A true individualism would presuppose a paramount interest in permitting the fullest possible development of individual life. If such a true individualism begins to be achieved, that which defeats individuality in our present system will increasingly be made to disappear.

OVERCOMING EXTREME INEQUALITY

This is the first requirement: that for the profit-making motive there be substituted the motive of fulfilling life. We pass now to the second. It will doubtless be necessary, in a society that is to release individual life in fullest degree, that the outstanding foe of free and generous individual development be removed. This foe is extreme inequality of income. We are so habituated to such extreme inequality that we have almost lost the power to detect its demoralizing effects. Indeed, we go in the opposite direction and sing pæans in praise of inequality as a necessary incentive to ambition and progress. If it were indeed such a necessary incentive, we should doubtless have to retain it, for stagnation can hardly be an acceptable social goal. But one doubts whether the reasons given in support of the kind of inequality of income that prevails are anything more than rationalizations after the facts. One does not hear the dispossessed singing these praises. Invariably they are sung by those who have done well for themselves, and who, quite obviously, are gratified by their own superior place in the order of things human.

What we do easily perceive is that, progress or no progress, extreme inequality of income is the source of most of the attitudes and behaviors that make man's life a sorry picture. Envy, over-reaching, lick-spittling, double-dealing, desire for revenge, keeping up with the Joneses, the surrender of one's integrity—all of these are born of a world in which some have a great deal and others have very much less. Extreme inequality of income makes the striving for money an obsession of present-day individuals, so that all other values become incidental. It makes it possible for them easily and consciencelessly to go the way of crime in the effort to raise themselves to a higher level of monetary power. But above all, it distorts the social vision, so that, for the most part, people are unable to see the human issue clearly. If they possess, they wish to hold on to what they have; if they do not possess, they wish the overturn of the possessors. In almost no case is there the power to see life steadily and whole in terms of its essential problems and possibilities.

The tale of the evils that lurk in extreme inequality of income would be long in the telling. It becomes increasingly clear, however, as we view our money-concentrated world, that some stimulus must be found other than such inequality if progress is not to be merely a more or less continuous effort to lift oneself above others at the cost of these others. What we seem to be wanting is some new, more generous way of life, where the motivations shall be intrinsic and where success shall not be estimated by the distance which one moves above the monetary levels of others, but rather by the degree to which one uses one's valid powers and assists the advance of one's whole society.

MEANS FOR ACCOMPLISHING THIS

The first requisite, if we are to move away from the disturbing inequality which now prevails among us, is, once more, a change of attitude. We shall have, no doubt, to generate a new form of disgust—disgust at fortunes that are far beyond the levels of any conceivable human wants. At the present time, the prevailing attitude is one not of disgust but of envy—an attitude which indicates quite clearly that despite wide protestations against social injustice, most individuals are tarred by the same brush. They would all, if they could, have what a few now possess. A maturely moral society will be one in which the very thought of large fortunes will elicit the same kind of disgust as is elicited by an act of boorishness or poor sportsmanship. When we become vividly aware of the demoralizing qualities bred in a society by the presence of extreme inequalities of income, we shall come to regard vast wealth not as a glory but as a shame.

Whenever and if ever this attitude develops, the way toward equalization of incomes will easily be open. There is first of all, as we have pointed out, even now the way of a steeply graduated income tax. Once we sincerely wish to rid ourselves of vast accumulations of private wealth, this will be a ready means for accomplishing what we desire. There is, in the second place, the way of a higher wage. Combined with the taxation of fortunes, this would go far toward the equalizing of incomes. There is also a third way already referred to, that of increase in public wealth. People do not always recognize that an increase in public wealth means an increase in their private incomes. But one easily realizes that every satisfactory access which the individual has to the use of public agencies means an increase in his income. For income, after all, is nothing but opportunity; and when opportunities are extended by the various forms of public wealth, incomes are thereby extended.

There will doubtless in good time be other ways discovered. It may be that we shall eventually advance to the stage in which all the means of production and distribution will be publicly owned. Then extreme inequalities of income would easily be disposed of. What the income distribution would be under such conditions is quite beyond our present powers to anticipate. In this matter, we shall probably have to learn by doing, and it would therefore be folly to attempt to prophesy too far ahead. But we may be assured that once a disapproving attitude is taken toward extreme inequality of income, we shall move toward such an organization of life as will open more fully the opportunities of life to every member of society.

THE PROBLEM OF YOUTH

We pass now to a further requirement. Curiously enough it is one to which little thought is given. When, however, we realize that any society which is to be just to its members must be made up of individuals who are themselves just, the problem becomes a pressing one. It is necessary, in other words, if a socialized society is to be achieved, that there be socialized individuals to achieve it.

At the present time we are in a fairly unsatisfactory condition. We speak, rather valiantly and hopefully, of making good citizens of our children; but when we are frank with ourselves—or better, when we dispel our prevailing sentimental illusions about citizenship—we realize that we continually fail.

Perhaps the chief source of our failure lies in the fogginess of our thought as to what we mean by good citizenship. Do we mean by a good citizen one who is trained to perpetuate the present order of things; or do we mean one who realizes his fullest possibilities as a human creature and who is interested in assisting others in like manner to realize theirs? Obviously the former meaning is far too narrow for a progressive society, and yet, in large measure, it is the meaning implied in most of our training for citizenship. When our young people cease to be young and take the government of life in their hands, they, following our instruction, proceed in turn to perpetuate the same inadequate conception of citizenship. And so, with the best of intentions, we train our youth to prevent the world's becoming any better than it is.

We do more than this. We—quite unwittingly, no doubt, but effectively—condemn our youth to a kind of spiritual poverty. The young man or woman in the school or college is given no opportunity to look forward to anything save to a life of self-interested enterprise. The whole emphasis of our civilization is upon the concept of establishing a place for oneself in the economic and social sun. The thought which the young person constantly meets—in the home and in the schoolroom—is that he is preparing himself to make the most of himself and for himself. Nowhere is any proper opportunity given to him for the development of generous social attitudes and behaviors. He is trained, in short, for the pursuit of life for himself.

William James felt this very keenly, and in an essay of remarkable penetration he suggested what he called a "moral equivalent for war." In war-time the individual transcends his ego-centered self. In swift, dramatic ways he responds to the call of the group. So powerfully does he feel that call and so eager is his response that he yields his comfort and even the safety of his life for values that go quite beyond his self-centered interest. James had no liking for war, but he had a liking for this ego-transcending experience, and he asked why society in its times of peace could not provide opportunities of a similar kind for the release of young people into wider and more generous responses. He suggested the enlistment of all young people for the term of a year or more in public work of various kinds—building roads, clearing out swamp-lands, reforesting, and, in the case of young women, nursing the sick, teaching children, assisting in the work of the camps.

We are well enough aware that individuals in a group become capable of attitudes and behaviors which they are unable to generate by themselves. This is well attested by our belief in the value of organizations like those of the Boy Scouts and Camp Fire Girls. Hitherto we have utilized the psychological effect of group-life chiefly in military ways. Is it not possible, James asked, to develop a fine group-mindedness through the enlistment of young people in a type of service that will not only give them an honorable place in our midst, but also satisfy their own youthful desires for a kind of rough adventurousness of life?

Undoubtedly James was right, and we shall not advance very far until we seriously make the effort to pass beyond our present ego-centering education of youth, so that when they take the government of affairs into their own hands, they may see, a little more clearly than we, how life is to be built on a pattern of wide social participation.

CONTROL OF BIRTH

There is another matter that has serious bearing on the future. We have already indicated the disastrous effect of a *laissez faire* attitude in economics and have shown the need for advancing to a rational control of industrial and commercial processes. It is not always realized that a similar attitude of *laissez faire* has prevailed with regard to reproduction. Indeed it is startling to contemplate the extent to which we have operated on the official theory that in matters of child-bearing man should abnegate his intelligence and let Nature have full sway. That this is the official theory is indicated by the fact that any sincere and intelligent effort to instruct married people in the art of bearing children according to planned desire is regarded in our own country as illegal and subject to severe punishment. Legally, in short, we are bidden to let come what may. Whereas in every other region of existence the way is opened—or at least not barred—for the application of intelligence to the enterprises of life, in this most vital of all areas, intelligence is strictly forbidden to enter. Law, in other words, stamps with its approval the old superstition that children come at the will of higher powers and that any intervention of human reason is a sacrilege and an obscenity.

Obviously no true release of life can be achieved until the difficult problem of population is settled. There can be no fine flowering of life where children come swarming as the by-products of sexual passion, unwanted and unprepared for.

It is astonishing, when one thinks of it, that despite our long residence on the planet, we have not yet achieved an intelligent mastery of the most intimate of all our functions. Throughout the ages reproduction has been, and still in large measure remains, a major mystery. Nevertheless, practically all peoples have realized the disastrous effects of an uncontrolled birth rate and have tried in one way or another to prevent overpopulation. They have practiced infanticide and abortion, mutilation of the sex organs, and in rare cases, celibacy. War and pestilence have been kindly aids in this process of helping an ignorant and bewildered humanity to stem the tide of reproduction.

Doubtless the day is at hand when reproductive *laissez faire* is to be succeeded by intelligent control of childbearing. Biological and medical science have made notable advances during the past centuries; indeed they may be said to have entered for the first time into effective relation to man's life. Also, there is an increasing sense of the value of voluntary and considered parenthood as well as of the wholesomeness of families small enough to give each child a chance for parental companioning and life-opportunity. Likewise there is a rapid diminution of the fatalistic supernaturalism of the religions and a growing wish to submit even the hitherto mysterious processes of conception and birth to intelligent exploration and control.

In the effort to rid ourselves of poverty, vice, crime, pestilence, and war, control of birth is a prime necessity. In the early nineteenth century, Malthus pronounced his famous word of warning, but he himself, overawed by the traditional morality, was too timid to draw the conclusions from his own premises. Bolder spirits, however, saw the clear pointing of his argument. As long ago as 1818, John Stuart Mill formulated the challenge to the old superstitions: "The grand practical problem," he said, "is to find the means of limiting births."

It still remains a "grand practical problem." Unfortunately much of the hindrance to its solution has come from laws sponsored by elements in the community inimical to the extension of scientific intelligence into regions hitherto under the government of supernatural authority. Thus the researches that might otherwise have advanced us far in the direction of discovering means of wholesome birth-spacing have been largely estopped, and the whole matter has been left, in the main, to scientifically ignorant politicians and laymen. Nevertheless the movement for the application of intelligence to this profoundly vital matter has grown stronger with the years, and there is reason to hope that in no very long time the senseless restrictions that now prevail will be removed, so that we shall be able to turn our scientific minds seriously to the task of finding out how man may be master of this very essential part of his fate. For it remains true that no far-reaching liberation of life can be effected, and no progressive bettering of the human stock, until the processes of reproduction are taken out of the region of supernaturalism and legal conservatism and given their place within the areas of man's intelligent inspection and control.

SOCIALIZING THE ECONOMIC ORDER

After these excursions, we return again to economic matters, for the chief and captain of our difficulties continues to lie in the economic process itself. We need not repeat what we have already said at sufficient length about self-interest being no adequate motive for a highly civilized society. It will readily be granted, then, that a major requirement of life is to move forward toward an economic system that has a social motivation.

We see this already taking place in a number of ways. To be sure, we are still largely in a state of economic war. Trades unions fight with employers for advances in wage, and employers fight with trades unions for reductions in wage. But in the midst of the bitter fighting, there are movements of economic life that would already seem to be pointing in a new direction.

CONSUMERS' COÖPERATION

Chief of these, perhaps, is the type of movement that goes by the name of consumers' coöperation. Consumers have learned to coöperate in order to eliminate the worst of the evils arising out of a competitive profit-making system. It is notable that where the movement of consumers' coöperation is strong—as in England—social ideals prevail. Thus there is the significant provision that however much an individual may own of the stock of a coöperative enterprise, he may have but one vote, on the principle that not money but man shall govern. For in a typically capitalistic enterprise, a man's power is in proportion to his stockholding investment. In capitalism, it has come to pass that money has increasingly ruled human life, and as it has gained in power, it has dominated with an increasing disregard of any interests save those of gain.

In the second place, the basic principle of consumers' coöperation is that goods shall be produced for use and not for profit. To that end all available surplus is turned back to the participators in the enterprise, either in dividends or in forms of shareable wealth. The latter disposition of surplus has a significant place in the movement. For a coöperative society is more than a mere business enterprise; it is a social one as well, since part of the available surplus is invariably used for the educational and recreational good of its members.

Finally, consumers' coöperatives cast out utterly that ugliest of all the practices found widespread in a profit-making régime, the practice of deception as to the quality of the goods sold. Since the members sell to themselves there is no point in deceiving themselves. Hence at one stroke the ugliness of extravagant and deceptive advertising and the foisting of inferior goods upon unwary purchasers are eliminated and life moves with the confidence of an acceptable commercial honesty.

THE OUTLOOK

When we realize that the coöperative enterprise, which started its modern career about ninety years ago with a few poverty-stricken weavers and a wheel-barrow, at the present time includes from seventy to eighty millions of members in thirty-six countries, we are constrained to believe that there is something in the movement not easily to be defeated. When we further realize that the very essence of the movement lies in complete repudiation of the profit-making principle, we are given hope that the wider socialization of economic enterprise is not an impossible dream.

Indeed we are the more heartened when we become aware that consumers' coöperation has been able to advance to the stage where it is not only a selling agency but a producing one as well, for many coöperatives own and run their farms and factories. In England, for example, in 1929, the retail societies produced goods to the value of £36,806,000 and the two wholesale to the value of £37,139,000. Here, indeed, were enterprises sufficiently vast to put an economic principle to the severest test. Despite all the complexities involved in production, however, the coöperatives were able to perform productive services for themselves with complete effectiveness.

Coöperatives have even advanced into the region of banking, thus freeing themselves of the control of capitalistic finance, and it is not unlikely that there will soon be effected an international coöperative bank to serve the interest of coöperatives throughout the world. In this way the principle of coöperation will be given its opportunity to overleap the boundaries of nations and knit peoples together in the primary processes of serving life through socialized forms of production and distribution.

PRODUCERS' COÖPERATION

There is another form of socialized economic enterprise which has sprung out of the wish of producers to join themselves together in a joint enterprise and thereby liberate themselves from the tyrannies and wastes of the capitalistic system. Such coöperation has had various success, depending in large measure upon the degree to which the self-interest of the members could be educated into social interest. One of the most significant forms of such coöperation is found in cases where a factory is completely owned and operated by its workers. Here the workers elect their superiors, set their wage scale, organize their work schedules, and carry on all the essential business of the enterprise.

One remarkably successful and high-minded experiment along this line is William Hapgood's conserve factory in Indianapolis, Indiana. The interested reader will find an account of it in Devere Allen's "Adventurous Americans." He will be particularly impressed by the surprising way in which latent qualities of management have been developed in the worker-owners and by the spirit of good sportsmanship permeating the whole concern. Indeed, he will doubtless think wistfully of the far different spirit manifested where workers are hired men only and where another body of people, the owners, operate chiefly in the interest of their own financial gain.

CAPITALISM SOCIALIZES ITSELF

Even within enterprises strictly capitalistic, however, we find movements toward the socializing of human relationships. While these movements only scratch the surface of the difficulties generated by a profit-making régime, they nevertheless indicate the way in which the wind is blowing. The old principle of "the worker be damned," like that of "the public be damned," is rapidly being superseded by the conviction that a decently prosperous enterprise must be decent both to its workers and to its public. No doubt this concern both for worker and public has not been born out of any disinterested motivation. Nevertheless, as attention becomes concentrated upon the welfare of the worker and upon honest service to the public, the day approaches more rapidly when the major uglinesses of a competitive, profit-making system will be eliminated, and business and industry will be prepared to undertake that profounder and more far-reaching socialization which will be necessary if the present order is to be changed into one more acceptable.

An outstanding example of the socializing relationships within industry is found in the case of the Amalgamated Clothing Workers of America. "Twenty years ago," writes Earl Dean Howard, "it was one of the most chaotic of industries, with a most unsavory reputation for the exploitation of its workers in notorious sweatshops. Now it ranks high as an industry in which standards are maintained, and the workers have attained a high degree of self-respect." [1]

[1] Earl Dean Howard; *Economic Problems of Tomorrow;* in *Society Tomorrow,* page 48; edited by Baker Brownell. Courtesy of D. Van Nostrand Company, publishers.

Through the leadership of Mr. Sidney Hillman, of the Amalgamated Clothing Workers Union, a joint control was effected by means of an impartial chairman and a board of arbitration in each area of the industry. The function of the impartial chairman (selected jointly by employers and union employees) has been to pass judgment upon industrial conflicts as they arise. The function of the board of arbitration has been to interpret and enforce these agreements and to be a final arbiter in the adjustments of all disputes.

This arrangement has had notable effects. In the first place, it has stabilized the industry by placing at the disposal of both parties a recognized procedure for the settlement of conflicts. In the second place, it has given to the workers what amounts to property-rights in their jobs. According to the agreement, no worker can be discharged without a full review of his case by the impartial chairman, and, if appeal be taken, by the board of arbitration. In the third place, it has made possible an equitable stabilization of working hours. If the volume of work diminishes, the number of jobs is maintained and each worker works shorter hours. If the job is abolished by reason of manufacturing changes, the worker has a claim upon another that is as near like it as possible. In addition, there is an unemployment insurance fund amounting to three per cent of the pay roll—each party contributing one and one-half per cent.

But what is most notable of all, this arrangement has made possible the building up of a body of industrial law outside the recognized regions of legislation and litigation and has thereby enabled this industry to be both the maker of law for itself and the governor of its own procedures in behalf both of employers and employees.

There are many other instances of the humanizing of relationships within industry. In many cases, to be sure—as in the notorious American Plan—they have been but thinly veiled attempts to outlaw the unions and to gain a complete control of labor through puppet organizations of workers. But on the whole it may be said that there are definite trends toward a socialization of industrial relationships. While such socialization is still far from what might be desired, it is so far in advance of the earlier forms of economic domination that it gives hope for a still more satisfactory future.

BEYOND NATIONALISM

There is one more major requirement if the release of life which we are contemplating is to be achieved. There will be needed an effective socialization of the world. At the present time, nations operate on the principles of a kind of refined banditry. The result is that life is everywhere insecure and a vast enginery of armies and navies saps the productive energies of mankind. No very great advance can be made toward the adequate liberation of life until the military and diplomatic barbarisms still inherent in the organization of the world are removed.

Nationalism exhibits a peculiar irrationality in the manner in which it makes impossible the wise organization and use of the materials at the disposal of man. Raw materials found in one country are held for the special benefit of the economic enterprisers of that land. Nations without appropriate raw materials must pay toll to the financial overlords of other nations. In the most exasperating ways the world of natural resources is divided up, and economic groups, backed by the armies and navies of their land, compete with other economic groups, backed by the armies and navies of their land.

In a healthy organism the whole is always greater than the sum of its parts. In our world life, on the contrary, the parts are greater than the whole, for each part has it within its power to frustrate not only the welfare of other parts but to make impossible an organized sanity which is the essential of world unity.

The whole situation is a kind of international madness that periodically involves man in the blackest of tragedies whose shadows are cast over succeeding generations in the form of prodigious taxes for the payment of old wars and the preparation of new ones. Also, it develops throughout the world attitudes of suspicion, fear, and hatred that make impossible a generous experimenting with human relationships on a large scale and that prolong the reign of the political patrioteer and the international racketeer.

The principle of exclusive self-interest which operates in the economic area has operated likewise among the nations of the world. Each, as sovereign, has been, in chief measure, the arbiter of its own destiny; and each, quite unblushingly, has pursued its own welfare as its major objective. If self-interest is altogether too low a motive for individual life, it does not become less low by the aggregating of individuals into nations. Obviously, then, human life will not come into its own until the self-interest of nationhood is transformed into the public interest of a world society.

CONCLUSION

The drama of human history is that of the successive uncovering of what human life has in it to be. We stand today at the threshold of a new uncovering. We believe as never before in the right of the individual to the development of the powers that lie within him and to the fulfillment of interests that are valid for himself and for his society. A future civilization, no doubt, will accept as its profoundest obligation the release of these powers and interests of individuals. To this end, it will seek to eliminate the injustice of extreme inequalities of income; it will save its youth from the spiritual poverty of a mere seeking for self; it will give scope for the application of intelligence to the control of child-birth; it will socialize its economic processes; and it will internationalize its world. Such a civilization may still be long in coming, but there are signs that it is already on the way.

PART II

RETHINKING WHAT WE HAVE ACCEPTED

". . . an inflexible and hasty nation
That sees already done
Rather too much that has not yet begun."
EDWIN ARLINGTON ROBINSON—*Dionysus in Doubt*

CHAPTER 5. OUR CHANGED MENTALITY

PROMISED lands are not reached in a day. In a world like our own, where thinking has hardened into habit, and where institutions have taken on a relative fixity of form, progress from the old to the new can be accomplished only in the face of much mental and emotional resistance. Old mind-sets have to be resolved into a hospitable flexibility in order that new attitudes and expectancies may be formed. This takes time. The children of Israel, as we remember, were compelled to wander for a long span of apparently fruitless years in order, no doubt, that their slave-bound minds might have time to grow into the needed patterns of independence and resourcefulness.

The promised land into which we are seeking entrance is one in which there will be intelligent control of resources for the common welfare. Have we, today, minds capable of entering such a promised land?

When we think of the low motivation and the unintelligent wastefulness that our system has involved, we are inclined to answer in the negative. But our self-distrust is doubtless excessive. Important changes have taken place in our mental make-up, but they have occurred so gradually that we have, for the most part, failed to take note of them. However, an analysis of what has happened to ourselves within the past few decades reveals that we are today a very different folk from what we formerly were. For this difference we may thank the very profit-economy whose passing away we are now happily anticipating.

TECHNOLOGICAL MINDEDNESS

It is obvious, in the first place, that we are today a people accustomed to technological expertness. We are not surprised at inventions which involve a degree of scientific knowledge and technological skill undreamed of in former ages. For this widespread scientific and technological expertness the profit-economy is responsible. In the effort to find new goods to sell, it has pushed its enterprises into more and more complicated regions of manufacture. It has called for the services of science and technological skill; and as it has called for them, it has released the latent powers of discovery and invention.

In the older centuries, the average mind took it for granted that things were to be accomplished chiefly by the power either of violence or of magic. War and supernatural religion were the preëminent techniques of life. Today both of these are being rapidly discredited. If, in this twentieth century, we wish to better our condition, we no longer think first of descending upon defenseless neighbors or of calling the attention of some god to our pressing needs. We look about for a scientist or an inventor—in short, for an individual trained to operate in the region of causes and effects.

Indeed, our confidence in this kind of cause-effect

operating individual is so great that it begins to diminish our confidence in another kind of individual. In former centuries, we placed a large measure of our trust in the political leader. We found him artful in eloquence, and we followed him because of his superior persuasiveness. Today we have developed a growing distrust of political leaders. The reason is not far to seek. Political leaders, for the most part, are not disinterested and technically equipped seekers after the truth. Rather, they are, in general, professional persuaders who seek power for themselves. A century of scientific and technological advance has taught us that true success in the handling of life-situations is to be achieved not through a kind of slippery persuasion but through the arduous processes of observation, experimentation, and rigorous verification.

This is why, in the present day, we stand a good deal dismayed before our legislatures and parliaments. What help can come from these crowds of partisan and undisciplined minds? In a world of bewildering complexity, we now feel that the government of life must be achieved through the instrumentality of a different kind of individual.

All this, no doubt, is to the good. We are at last prepared in our minds for a reconsideration of the government of life. Traditional habits of ready acceptance have been broken, and we are, in a sense, expectant of a new order of political life based on the rigorous and disinterested use of intelligence. Two developments, then, have occurred: (1) a confidence in the scientific and technological approaches to life; (2) a skepticism as to traditional governmental forms and procedures. These are no small achievements. They provide us with both a destructive and a constructive preparation for the future.

ORGANIZING POWER

There has been a further achievement. As the manufacture and sale of goods have grown at accelerated speed, we have learned to organize machinery and man-power into larger and more complex units. To be sure, we have suffered our failures. At times, our huge structures, built upon shifting financial sands, have collapsed; but on the whole, the past few decades have witnessed a remarkable success in the integration of small operative units into larger.

We are not interested here in the financial aspect of this type of development but in its psychological consequences. We have, in short, learned to think in larger areas. In matters of widespread organization, the word impossible is less and less in use. To think of a business that is nation-wide in its scope is nowadays a commonplace. Even to think of a business as world-wide in its organization is almost a commonplace.

This change in our mentality, too, is of no small moment. If we are to move into a more highly socialized order of life, organization over wide areas will be necessary. Doubtless we are on the threshold of world-organization. It is important, then, that the contemplation of enterprises nation-wide and world-wide shall give us no terrors. As long as we faced the future with provincial minds, we could not proceed far in the world-wide organization of life that a new order of civilization requires. But we are increasingly less provincial in mind. Even the most average individual today lives in a kind of world-area. We have, in short, moved out of our narrow territories, and, to this extent at least, we are ready for the overpassing of boundaries that unduly hinder the wider integration of our existence.

CULTURAL ENRICHMENT

Only a few decades ago most lives were deplorably meager in their opportunities to draw upon the resources of the arts, literatures, and sciences. Outside a few large cities, life was lived in a kind of cultural waste-land. This does not mean that there were not, here and there, individuals who generated a kind of wise culture out of themselves and the few opportunities at their command. But it does mean that the average life was culturally barren. I can myself remember, as a lad, visiting my uncle's farm in California and finding myself limited to the simple music that one of my cousins could evoke in a precarious attack upon a wheezy old melodeon. Even at that, "God Save the Queen" and "The Blue Bells of Scotland" were a joy to my boyish soul. Today, on that same farm, a symphony can be plucked out of the air. Music, of a richness undreamed of in my boyhood days, is daily at command.

To be sure, other things of less moment are likewise at command, and it is true that people today mingle the great offerings indiscriminately with all the trivialities that the vibratory spaces are made to suffer. Nevertheless, anyone who has been at all observant knows that music of a high order has become a part of the everyday life of thousands of people who formerly were compelled to be without it. That it has had an enriching effect upon the emotional life of these people there can be no doubt, for that is precisely what great music does.

Radios and phonographs have not been placed upon the market with the conscious intent of enriching lives. They have been placed there in order to make profits. But here again the profit-making economy has produced a result far finer than its conscious purpose. The same may be said of the wide distribution of books and magazines. While easy access to printed matter has in many cases produced minds ready to absorb but too indolent to digest, and while much of the reading matter is not worth the perusing, this wide distribution of books and magazines has opened many a door that hitherto has been closed.

The same is true with regard to reproductions of paintings and sculpture. I have on my own walls colored reproductions of a number of modern masterpieces. To be sure, these reproductions are not the originals, and I might be regarded as crude in taste for my willingness to be satisfied with copies. But the originals are not only in foreign lands but completely beyond the range of my financial capacity. I feel no humiliation in having these copies on my walls, for they are remarkably true to the originals, and they permit me to have a kind of commerce with masters whom otherwise I should have slight chance of knowing.

The case is typical of what is true throughout our contemporary society. In the humblest homes, great artists are no longer denied entrance. We recall the hideous prints that were the only resource of our forefathers—the petrified crayon portraits, the woodeny dogs, the sentimental ladies sitting in sylvan glades. Our forefathers did the best they could, but no profit-economy had yet speeded up its processes to produce at a low cost reproductions of the masterpieces of the world.

There is a significance in this that is not generally noted. Minds crude in taste and undiscriminating in appreciation can hardly serve to build a noble civilization. It is therefore of singular moment that the profit-economy, in placing the riches of art, science, and literature at our command has enabled our minds to grow in sensitiveness to the true and the beautiful. When the profit-economy stands at the gate of Heaven, begging for entrance into Paradise, this at least will have to be said in its favor: that, despite the vulgarization which it effected in its mercenary stimulation of many of our lower impulses, it nevertheless made possible for millions of us access to the triumphs of man's spirit, and in so doing raised the level of our appreciations.

URBANITY

The profit-economy, in congregating people together, has at least taught them increasingly how to live together. Those who travel much on trolley-cars and subways learn the art of restraining their crude impatience, of controlling the rugged individualism that would bid them elbow their way through crowds to the hurt of weaker members. A city street swarming with people is an example of the kind of considerateness that crowded juxtaposition demands. The typical city man learns to insinuate himself through a mass of people with swiftness and without affront to his neighbors.

It is significant to note the kind of courtesy of the road that has developed since the advent of motor cars. This courtesy, to be sure, is in large measure a matter of one's own safety; yet it develops beyond a mere crudeness of self-interest into a give-and-take of the road. Such terms as "road-hogs," "speed-devils," "hit-and-run drivers" are sufficiently indicative of the kind of condemnation which is visited upon those who have not learned the lessons of road courtesy and consideration.

In the last few decades, eating away from home has become an increasingly widespread custom. Looked upon first askance, as something that would inevitably destroy the delicacies bred within the home, it has turned out to be a developer of manners. When a man takes his family to a restaurant or hotel dining room, he is not likely to sit in suspendered ease nor to shout disparaging remarks at his wife and children. Indeed, it may be said that where every man's home is his dining room, manners are likely to be far cruder than where individuals perform their food rites in the observant presence of their fellows.

Thus we note the paradoxical fact that the very crowding of life which an aggressvie industrialism has effected and which is so often deplored as destructive of the admirable graces of older days, has, despite its shortcomings, developed a new courteousness among us—that of people who, in their enforced aggregatings, have learned the art of mutual accommodation and of a more or less generous considerateness.

There is, again, a significance in this. If we are to advance to a highly socialized civilization, we shall have to learn the art of living together. But that art has already, in some measure, been learned. Hence we need not fear that further socialization will find us unready. We are even now a partly socialized people, and further steps in the direction of a closer unity of life may be taken without the loss of qualities too precious to be surrendered.

THE ART OF KEEPING WELL

If one examines the advertisements in a subway or trolley-car, one notes the large proportion of them that have to do with keeping clean and well. One remembers the melancholy tales of young gentlemen and young ladies who have failed to realize the deadly effects of bodily odors, or of those who, having neglected properly to brush their teeth, are fated to belong to a certain notorious "four out of five." We recall the pictures of luscious oranges which remind us that several glasses of orange juice per day will provide the body with needed vitamins. We are frequently amused at it all. Sometimes we are irritated at downright misrepresentation. But on the whole, it may be said that advertising such as this has accomplished the result of making us health-conscious.

It is only a very crabbed soul who will deny the value

of this. After all, bodily health is a prerequisite to most of the sanities, and a society taught by its advertisers how to keep fit is in so much better position not only to believe in a life of fitness-for-all but to move forward to mental and social health. The most deplorable aspect of many countries that have not received the blessings as well as the curses of the profit-economy is the large amount of filth and bodily decrepitude.

We may therefore set it down as an asset of no small value that the profit-economy, in its aggressive sales campaigns, has made us anxious and able to keep ourselves both clean and healthy. If we are indeed passing out of an inadequate past into a more civilized future, such widespread sensitiveness to cleanliness and health will not be without its value.

THE PROLONGATION OF YOUTH

There is another effect of the profit-economy which is of importance. We have already referred to the technological expertness required for the invention and manufacture of articles of sale. The need for such expertness has had an unexpected result. In former centuries, a young man entered upon his life-work at a relatively early age. If he was to be a farmer, he already possessed the knowledge requisite for his vocation while still little more than a lad. If he was to be a tradesman, there was little that he was required to understand which could not be learned in a few years of adolescent apprenticeship. If he was to be a lawyer, the law of his simple society could be learned in a relatively short space of time. The same was true of the would-be physician, teacher, or minister of religion. There was no need for a protracted period of training. Almost with the casting off of childish things, the boy became a man, equipped to take up a man's work. It will be remembered that Shakespeare represents Hotspur as a general of troops while still in his teens.

The serious business of life began early. However, a significant change has occurred. The knowledge now requisite for the technological pursuits, and for law, medicine, and even business, requires a protracted period of training. Hence it is no longer possible to take off the bib and produce the man. After the bib must come years of training in high school, college, and university before the young man (and now the young woman) is ready to take up the responsible business of adulthood.

This has resulted in an unprecedented development of education. The years of youth have been prolonged, and a vast enginery of schooling has been built up to occupy the prolonged years with the securing of knowledge and expertness.

John Fiske pointed out that the trait which most distinguishes man from the lower animals is prolongation of infancy. This trait is important, according to him, because of the opportunity which it gives for a period of flexibility and learning. Animals quickly assume the stereotyped forms of their adult world and so are unable to make progress. Man, on the contrary, gifted with the privilege of living through years of childish weakness, is enabled to utilize these years for the quiet unfolding and the slow maturing of the mind.

Obviously, then, the prolongation of youth must have consequences equally important. Through it more time is given for the absorption of the sciences and cultures, more time for experiments with ideas and for an orientation in the life-processes. Instead of being required to take a few hasty mouthfuls of the knowledge and culture available and be on to the business of making a living, the modern young person is given a span of years in which to nourish himself richly upon what the ages, in their triumphs, have handed to us.

To be sure, we are still babes at the task of educating. Much of what takes place in the schools and colleges ought never to take place. Nevertheless, with a kind of eagerness, we have come to believe in education, to want more of it and of better quality.

NEW EXPECTATIONS

Finally, the profit-economy has brought us this further benefit: it has made us less afraid of the new. Indeed, it has bred in us the habit of welcoming the new. This, of course, applies as yet chiefly to the realm of mechanical things. We are still, as ever, timid about social, political, and economic innovations. This was illustrated only recently by the request of a so-called American Patriotic Society that Albert Einstein be refused admission to America on the ground of his pacifistic affiliations. The ludicrous plea of the panic-stricken ladies could easily be paralleled by many another instance of senseless social timidity.

Nevertheless, a habit of welcoming the new has begun to be formed. In the realm of physical things, we have been trained, during the past few decades, to expect the still-better. Nor need we altogether despair as we contemplate our social and political timidities. A powerful movement against war is on foot among us. That is most significant, for never before in all man's history, save among a few outstanding spirits, and, at times, among the oppressed, has war been regarded as anything save a glorious necessity. A movement toward internationalism grows increasingly strong throughout the world. This, too, is of moment, for our most powerful emotions are still tied up with a restricted nationalism. Even in the region where we are apt to fight most tenaciously for established privileges—that of industry and finance—we have witnessed, as in Russia, the overthrow of an old order and the experimental establishment of a new type of economic society hitherto unknown among us; while in lands still operating on the traditional bases, we find a growing impatience with the ways of the past and a kind of bewildered demand for ways that are more adequate. Despite the obvious fact of social timidity, therefore, we do discover a kind of loosening up of minds, a kind of willingness to concede defects and to venture toward improvements. The profit-economy, in short, has, through its physical inventions, changed our habits so repeatedly that we have almost grown the habit of gladly changing our habits.

And so, unfortunate as our social inertia may still be, we are not so sadly off as we were in those centuries when generation followed generation without a single major change to give new direction to life. We are in the first stages of the development of the type of mentality requisite for an intelligent society. For intelligence is essentially the power to meet and master new situations.

THE OLD GIVES BIRTH TO THE NEW

"To know that one is in a prison," Edward Caird used to say, "is already to be outside the prison." Such a statement might be met with a wry face by an individual condemned to pass his days behind prison bars. And yet there is truth in it. One might express it in this way: to feel the irksomeness of a situation is already to be in a mental condition for overcoming that irksomeness. If we were all well satisfied with the world in which we live, there would be little hope of our advancing toward any other kind of a world.

There is a curious paradox, then, in the profit-economy. It may be briefly expressed as follows: the more assiduously the profit-economy works for its own survival, the more surely it accomplishes its own elimination. Or, to express it differently, the profit-economy has within itself the seeds of its own self-transcendence.

The reason for the paradox is not far to seek. The object of a profit-economy is to make profits. In order that there may be profits, there must be goods to sell and customers to buy them. The goods that are sold must not be of a nature to do widespread harm to the buyers, else there will soon be no buyers. On the contrary, they must be of a nature to raise the level of the capacity of the buyers, for as this level is raised, the latter become better able to make purchases. Hence it is to the interest of a profit-economy not to depress the level of life of its customers but, on the contrary, to raise it.

This is precisely what has occurred. The profit-economy has, as it were, civilized life by introducing one ameliorating device after another. It has brought better housing, more adequate furniture, better textiles, more varied food, better sanitation. It has introduced new modes of locomotion, so that we have been less restricted to our localities. It has brought newspapers, magazines, and books. It has brought reproductions of paintings and sculpture. It has brought motor cars and roadways. Indeed, if we were to think back to the feudal days and contrast the condition of the average man in those days with that of the average man today, we should become aware of a significant transformation that life has undergone. It is sometimes asked, doubtingly, whether people are any happier today than they were in those earlier days. That question simply cannot be answered, as happiness is a subjective condition. But it is possible for us to say that a standard of living has been attained which was in no wise possible before the acceleration of production which began with the industrial revolution.

It is also possible to make another assertion. Man's mind, for the most part, grows in discriminating power with the variety of his experience. Let an individual have only a few unvarying experiences, and most of his power of discrimination remains undeveloped. Let him, however, pass through thousands of different experiences, and his power of discrimination tends to become increased.

This is exactly what has happened. With the very multiplication of the goods of life, man has achieved a variety of experiences which has enabled him to make more varied judgments than in the simpler, older days. That he has thereby grown in wisdom is not altogether certain. But that he has grown in the opportunity for exercising his judgment in many new ways is sure. Now he must grow in social responsibility as well.

THE REVOLT OF THE WRITERS

Perhaps the best indication of what has happened to the minds of many of us is found in the literary field. At no time in human history has there been the amount of passionate protest against the misuse of life that there is today. Here and there in the older literatures we find a brief word of pity for the underprivileged. But in general the literatures move on a level that is oblivious to the fact of human sufferings brought about by unjust or inadequate human arrangements. If we turn to Homer, we find a glorification of aristocratic life and a complete acceptance of the lot of the lowborn. In Euripides there are some swift words of pity, but one feels throughout his writings that the age had not yet arrived for a passionate concern with injustice to the lowly. Even in the social-minded Plato one finds only a device proposed whereby the drudges may be led to accept their drudgery. In the Oriental literatures it is not otherwise. Once in a long while one hears a plea for the worker, but in general, life is accepted as it is—a life of privileged masters and of underprivileged workers. Even Shakespeare's world is still the world of aristocrats. When he pictures the underprivileged man, he usually pictures him as a yokel, and uses him to draw forth our laughter.

But in the last few decades writer after writer has turned to this new theme—protest against man's inhumanity to man, condemnation of the sordidnesses, vulgarities, banalities of a society given over not to creative fellowship but to self-interested accumulation. What is most significant is that the severity of this protest has been sharpest in that land in which the profit-economy has come to its highest development—America. We remember how "Main Street" startled us into an awareness of the barrenness of a civilization that had supposed itself to be highly successful. We remember, too, how the figure of "Babbitt" made us suddenly aware of the kind of personality that our accelerated business enterprise had produced. We remember how Theodore Dreiser in his "Financier" drew the picture of financial ruthlessness. We recall Frank Norris's "Octopus," that tale of a devastating monopoly laying waste the hopes and energies of a gallant pioneering people. We recall Upton Sinclair's "Jungle," the tale of slaughterhouse barbarities that were as nauseating as the odors from that indescribable region of blood and filth. We recall the small-town stories of Sherwood Anderson, stories repeating the tale of an unimaginative civilization occupied with material accomplishments and unable to appreciate the individual whose mental and emotional life it frustrated.

We remember, too, the advent of a new kind of poetry in American life. Almost over night, we all began to read poetry, but poetry of a very different kind from that to which we had been accustomed in the Longfellows and Whittiers. Edgar Lee Masters wrote his "Spoon River Anthology," and instantly we were made aware of the festering poisons at work in a community typical of a civilization given over to the self-interest of money-making and material progress. More recently another poem has captured the imagination, not, indeed, of the greater part of the nation, but of many minds. T. S. Eliot's "Waste Land," bewildering, irritating, bizarre, is an attempted indictment of the vulgar incoherence of a civilization which has prided itself upon its achievements.

We remember the startling persuasiveness of Henry George's "Progress and Poverty" and the pathetic hopefulness of Bellamy's "Looking Backward." Here were no complacent glorifications of the *status quo*. Here were no satisfied beliefs in "manifest destiny" and the "white man's burden." Here were stinging indictments of an order that was mounting to its financial success on the backs of the defeated.

In recent years, all this passionate protest has been gathered up into a damning statistical survey, presented with a kind of soberness that is more powerful than passion. In "Middletown," we have been given the picture of a typical American city. It is not a pleasing picture, certainly not one to give us pride in any high value that we have achieved.

Whether this revolt of the writers is in every detail justified or not makes little difference. The significance of the situation lies in the fact of the revolt. But more significant even than the revolt itself, is the fact that it could not have occurred among a crude and unlettered people. It could only have occurred where the level of life had been raised to such a degree that new discriminations were possible. These very writers were themselves the products of the profit-economy. They had benefited by its manifold goods, they had read its books, gone to its schools, turned on its electric lights, ridden in its trains and motor cars—in other words, they were not the yokels of Shakespeare's day, but people who had received their training as the result of the wealth produced by a profit-economy, and whose discriminating minds were now able to turn against the crudeness of the very economy that produced them. Also they had readers, not only among the privileged superior ones, but among the mass of the average. They could write vigorously because they could be read understandingly.

So we come back to our paradox: the very system which multiplied the goods of life, produced minds which could turn against that system.

SOCIAL PROTEST

Precisely as there has never, in all history, been so widespread a spirit of social criticism among writers as during the past few decades, so likewise there has never been quite so widespread a demand for social reorganization. The movement known as socialism is typically an outcome of the capitalist régime. The labor movement in all its phases has been an effort of the exploited workers to gain some modicum of justice in a system where each man is for himself and the devil is supposed to take the hindmost. The very considerable development of consumers' coöperatives has been the effort to draw the fangs of a system which has had the common man too utterly at its mercy. The widespread opposition to war is the recognition of the fact that the lives of men should no longer be used as cannon fodder in behalf of irresponsible profiteers. Finally, the overturn of an age-old régime of aristocratic feudalism in Russia and the leaping over capitalism directly into communism is the indication that the modern consciousness has become too vividly aware of the shortcomings of the profit-economy to tolerate its presence when once the decks are swept clear for something new.

CONCLUSION

The foregoing tells enough of the story to make the point clear. A new kind of outlook has been developing among us. But this new outlook could not have been gained had there not occurred a lifting of the level of life. Not that the profit-economy aimed at any such result. But Saul went out to find his father's ass and gained a kingdom. The situation is not exactly parallel, to be sure, but it is suggestive. The profit-economy went out to find riches for itself and achieved new riches of life for us all. And now we, raised to a higher plane of understanding and intelligence, confront the profit-economy and ask that it move to a nobler level.

As we review the foregoing facts we come to a significant conclusion. What has happened to us in the past decades has been neither all good nor all bad. To those who can see only the bad, the profit-economy has been an unmitigated evil to be cast out root and branch. To those who can see only the good, the profit-economy has been a blessing to be maintained at all costs. The picture we have just drawn is perhaps in reality more reasonable. Also, it provides us with a very necessary hope. After all, what happens to us in the future must happen through the conscious purposings of men and women. No *deus ex machina* is to hand us the ideal society of the future. We ourselves, out of our own minds, are destined to shape whatever society is to be. Hence it is of no small consequence that our minds have already been turned in directions that are true. We need not retrace our steps. We have already grown familiar with much of the scenery that is to surround us in the future, and we are therefore already partly at home in the world that is to be.

CHAPTER 6. CONSIDERING THE PROBLEM OF CRIME

WHERE, on the one hand, as we have just seen, admirable qualities of mind have been developed by our profit-civilization, on the other hand, qualities far from admirable have been brought into existence. One of the things that deeply troubles us today is the rapid increase of crime. It is becoming a terrifying phenomenon. We live in a time when no one is safe against anti-social acts. Indeed, the very triumphs of our civilization have seemed to stimulate crime and to give it greater scope for operation. It is one of the bitterest commentaries upon our supposedly high grade civilization that crime is not only widespread but increasing.

Volumes have been written about the causation of crime, but the whole matter comes to a very simple truth. Few individuals are so mal-conditioned at birth that they are by nature criminals; practically all criminality is a product of the environment. Most of us know this; nevertheless we preserve an ancient attitude which makes crime root in some peculiar badness of nature. We still continue to believe that the way to deal with it is to do heavy punishing. The devil must be beaten out of the criminal, so that the latter may come forth clean. If we could understand the criminal as we understand a warped and shriveled tree, we should probably proceed differently. We should look to soil and sunshine.

An analysis of crime, in short, requires first of all an analysis of our civilization. Are there in it factors that might easily provide the kind of conditioning which would lead to crime? If so, can these be altered?

Crimes might be divided into two kinds: those of uncontrolled impulse—like crimes of anger, resentment, lust; and those of deliberate intention. Crimes of the first kind are relatively rare. It is the crimes of deliberate intention that bulk largest in our society and that are of the most pressing and continuous danger.

There is something profoundly significant about this. Deliberate intention presupposes a certain mind-set. The racketeer, for example, is not acting from impulse. He acts in terms of a developed habit of thought. He has deliberately chosen his way; he carefully plans his action; he carries it to execution with a considered effectiveness. He has, in short, come to a certain conclusion about life-relationships. He is not ashamed of that conclusion. He proceeds with a feeling of complete self-justification. If he is caught, he is not abased in his own mind. He has simply had a bad break.

The bootlegger is an almost respectable criminal who justifies his law-breaking on grounds that might seem to offer him much the best of the argument. He is a business man responding to the law of supply and demand. The forbidden thing is demanded; he is there to supply it. If he is caught, he shrugs his shoulders, pays his fine, and calls it a day.

The burglar—gentlemanly or otherwise—is a business man. He is getting as much as he can in as artful a way as he can. He trains himself to his task. He is an expert with his tools; he uses the devices of telephone and motor car. If he must shoot, it is unfortunate; but one must not permit the mere interests of others to stand in the way of one's own success.

The seller of worthless securities outlines his campaign and carries it to completion with careful ingenuity. He preys on the credulities and the mercenary propensities of his fellow men, and he easily justifies himself with the thought that the less clever are made to be exploited.

A gangster is a member of a corporation. He and his fellows have captured a monopoly, and they feel completely justified in preventing others from infringing upon their monopoly. To be sure, they have not gone through the recognized processes of lobbying and bribery to secure legislative recognition of their monopoly. They have simply captured it for themselves. But having captured it, they feel justified in defending their rightful property against all intruders.

TRACING TO CAUSES

Crime of this kind, in short, is not a kind of impulsive badness. It is, for the most part, coolly considered business. Any criminal with a fair degree of intelligence might make a good case for his particular form of enterprise on the ground that while it is not recognized by law, it is patterned on known business procedure.

It is easy to indulge in cynical exaggeration, since many modern business processes readily lend themselves to this. But quite without exaggeration it is possible to say that business at its lowest levels is a legally permitted process of getting as much and giving as little as possible.

There are two outstanding cynicisms that pervade our life today—one about politics and one about business. In each area, we tend to disbelieve in the genuineness of the expressed motives. As business and politics constitute the major areas of life, we might say that the prevailing attitude about life is cynical. The students in our schools very largely have this attitude. They know that life is not the virtuous, industrious, service-rendering process which their teachers frequently make it out to be. I have had students come back to me several years after they have graduated from college. They have talked of old times, have recalled the courses they took. "Those were great lectures you gave us, Professor; but . . ." I have come to know that "but" as a kind of reluctant, almost accusatory confession that while in college one might talk ardently of high ideals of human relationships, in the actual world one must do as the Romans do.

What do the modern Romans do? They manipulate the laws to their own advantage; they bribe officers of the law to do their bidding; they adulterate their goods; they falsify their advertising; they ask high prices for cheap patent-protected articles; they form conspiracies on the stock market with the intent of shearing the lamb; they issue inflated stocks; they give out exaggerated news to raise stock prices so that they may unload on the public;

they make mergers for the good of their pocketbooks and for the ill of the consumers. The spectacle of the president of one of our largest banks lecturing Tammany Hall on its derelictions and exploitations of public funds is made ridiculous in the light of his subsequent forced resignation facing charges of tax-dodging and the disclosure that he was a highly speculative Wall Street operator at a time when he had the responsibility for the administration of the funds of his depositors.

One of our educators has said recently that education and the profit-system cannot live together. As a matter of fact, education has solved the incompatibility in its own way. It has assumed, within the classroom, that there is essential virtue in the economic processes. But students know better; and knowing it, they enter the world of enterprise with eyes open for the likely chance. Indeed, it is not unusual to meet the kind of student who will say cynically: "Only saps work."

For this is the logical outcome of the each-for-himself philosophy. To get more for less is most successful when one can get everything for nothing. It is not a far cry, therefore, from the adulterator of goods to the snatcher of purses, or from the company that demands high tribute for its monopolized products to the racketeer who asks for his monthly contribution. Fundamentally they are all cut from the same cloth. Despite our belief that we live under the Mosaic Code, we actually, in large measure, live under a Spartan morality: "Steal, but don't get caught." I do not wish to appear to exaggerate, but it is difficult to distinguish between outright stealing and the less outright processes of taking from the buyer more than equitably should be taken; or giving to the buyer in return for his outlay that which is not what it is represented to be; or manipulating values so that they will appear to be more than they actually are; or giving to the worker less than he actually earns. What is stealing? It is taking what belongs to another without making an equitable return. All these processes come under this definition. They are, therefore, forms of stealing.

We are here, then, at the source of our difficulties. The prevailing processes of finance provide, as it were, the archetype; individuals, in one way or another, pattern themselves upon this archetype. Where the ways are made easy, individuals enter the ranks of high finance; where they are made difficult, they enter the ways of low finance. Crime, for the most part, is merely this kind of profit-economy operating without benefit of law.

COLLUSIVE AGREEMENT

This has been aptly illustrated by a recent writer who describes a new type of racketeering.[1] "A racket in these days must levy tribute not on small groups but on the massed millions who can't shoot back but who can be depended upon to provide a steady stream of gold. The syndicates have found such a money-maker.

" 'Get hold of the labor union.' That's the idea which the wise men of the syndicates have devised, and which they

[1] *If It Isn't Booze, It's Something Else,* by William G. Shepherd. *Collier's, The National Weekly* (November 26, 1932). Condensed in *Reader's Digest,* January, 1933.

are putting into force with gunmen, bombs, and threats. There was graft in father's booze; now there is to be graft in baby's milk. . . . It is sometimes difficult . . . for an employer to know if he is dealing with a real union or a union which has been seized by gangsters.

"When gangsters seize a union they usually decide, as a first measure, to cut the wages of the members. This suggestion not infrequently appeals to employers, so that they pay the 'union' for the service. A little later these same employers find a heavy tax levied on them for the use of a little window card. Bricks, or more likely bombs, will come through the show window if the card is not there. In this way the 'gangsterized union' gets its clutches on both the worker and the employer."

And then the writer goes on to make this significant analysis of the situation: "Make no mistake, business men in Chicago are not blameless for this new development. It is merely an outgrowth of the 'collusive-agreement racket' which has existed in Chicago for ten years.

"This 'collusive-agreement racket,' Colonel Robert Isham Randolph, head of Chicago Secret Six, told me, 'is comprised of four elements: the business man, the labor leader, the gangster, and the politician. The business man seeks to create a monopoly in his trade. He seeks, through misapplication of the law by politicians, or by the withdrawal of labor by union leaders, to drive his competitors from the field, so that he can maintain an artificially high price for his commodity. The labor leader seeks first a monopoly of control over the workmen engaged in a given trade, and then dispenses the right to work under the permit system at so much per man per day. The politician paralyzes the hand of the law, and looks for votes and money from the profits of the conspiracy. The gangster finds it lucrative employment to bomb, to commit arson, and to terrorize entire communities into staying away from the polls at election.

" 'In short,' says Colonel Randolph, 'this collusive-agreement racket is a combination of business, labor unionism, politics, and the criminal underworld that runs the whole gamut of crime, the purpose of which is exploitation through circumscribing the right to work and do business.' "

It is impossible any longer to put business into one category and crime into quite another. Business is itself the maker of crime to the degree that its processes are anti-social. Only when we clearly recognize this shall we be at the beginning of any effective movement to rid ourselves of crime.

WHAT SHALL WE DO?

Sparta lent no great lustre to Greece. She is now remembered as a state devoid of the qualities that make for a true culture. One wonders, at times, whether Western capitalism is not a kind of modernized Spartanism and whether it, too, will not pass into history as a civilization of artful rowdies.

Because the disease of crime is rooted in the average processes of our life, most of the suggestions as to what is to be done are beside the mark. In the article above quoted the writer asks: "How shall we deal with such rackets?"

This question is answered by Gordon L. Hostetter, Director of the Employers' Association, in a statement issued to Chicago business men. His answer goes not for Chicago alone, but for most of America:

"By recognizing, first of all, that crime in various forms has crept into the philosophy of American life today and must be rooted out—from fixing traffic tickets through the whole gamut of racketeering to the farthest reaches of fraudulent finance. Gangsterized industry is a symptom, and not the disease. It could not appear on the business surface without poisonous infection at work below." So far so good. But then comes the sentence which is typical of most American thinking, and which, like most of our thinking, misses the real issue. Says Mr. Hostetter: "The infection, the real disease, is the fact that we have shirked our responsibilities as citizens." By that, no doubt, he means that we have not gone to the polls with sufficient assiduity to make it possible that good men should be elected and severe laws should be passed preventing business malfeasance. But this falls far short of a realization of where the real issue lies. The real issue lies in the motivation involved in our profit-economy. As long as we are content to be a civilization based upon the principle of getting as much for ourselves and giving as little as possible, we have set a pattern for life which must inevitably produce chicanery and crime.

Life is now a more or less fierce effort to keep oneself alive. If the effort is not strenuous or artful enough, one may easily be defeated, with starvation as the ultimate of one's ill success. A very large proportion of criminals comes out of those ranks of life where poverty is constantly in evidence. They start life embittered. If they are intelligent, they turn their intelligence to ways of winning in the game of life. They have clear examples all around them of those who have not been stupid at the game but who, by clever devices, have won large prizes.

In his "Theory of the Leisure Class," Veblen showed the inevitable tendency of the poor to copy the rich in their modes of conspicuous display. The same tendency holds in the matter of getting a living: the poor copy the rich in their anti-social practices.

"Fear is the parent of cruelty," said Froude. Fear, we might say, is the parent of crime. The fear of destitution drives all of us to our various ways of guarding ourselves against defeat. But suppose no defeat were possible? Suppose that the decencies of life were available for all? Suppose that there were no ghastliness of poverty as an ever-present reminder of what might happen to ourselves if we were not clever enough to win at the game of life?

The elimination of poverty, one suspects, would be the sure way to the elimination of crime. Or, if not to its complete elimination, since the crimes of impulse would still remain, at least to such a diminution of it as would make a more livable world.

So it would seem that we need far more than to be good citizens, voting for "good men," pledged to "honesty" in the law. We need to be intelligent about the sources of crime, and to know that the "good men" whom we elect to office are, for the most part, citizens who not only support the present self-seeking order of things but who, in all good faith, operate in accordance with its accepted anti-social principles.

We require, in short, a system of life in which there is no possibility of poverty. Such a scheme of life, one suspects, can never be achieved until all the prime necessities are taken wholly out of the fluctuating region of finance. Today we battle for these prime necessities, and the victory goes to the artful and the strong. If there were no need for battling, life could, at least in this major region, achieve a serenity and a confidence that would render the typical ways of criminal self-seeking utterly pointless.

It is significant to note that in the regions where wealth has been made public there is no crime. One does not find racketeering groups of teachers, librarians, custodians of museums. The wealth within their control is free wealth. There is, therefore, no point in their organizing ways of holding up the users of this free wealth. In these regions, in short, life moves without fear and with a genuineness of motivation that can scarcely be found anywhere else in our modern world.

In the matter of crime, what is needed above all is a long view. We have tried all kinds of short views. But where the very atmosphere about us is heavy-laden with the poison of self-seeking motivation, and where the fear of destitution is ever-present, it is hopeless to expect the development of a genuinely wholesome life. No more than we can make a silk purse out of a sow's ear can we expect to make a social-minded citizenry out of a civilization in which anti-social practices are the accepted and expected order of the day.

CHAPTER 7. THE CHALLENGE TO EDUCATION

WHENEVER there is any long continued social difficulty, we hear people say: "Education will solve the problem." It is a kind of accepted patter—a curiously unfortunate kind, because it serves constantly to cloud the fundamental issue.

The fact is that there are many different kinds of education. There can be an education for thievery—subtle or crude. There can be an education which makes snobs of people—we have it in many of our finishing schools. There can be an education which makes a people feel itself superior to all other peoples. And also there can be an education which deepens comprehension and broadens outlook. In short, there can be good education and bad. Therefore to assert that education will make us over into acceptable human beings and solve all our problems is meaningless.

When one looks upon the average types of education, one must agree that, however much they have succeeded along certain lines, nevertheless, as to developing individuals trained to intelligent social-mindedness, they have been disappointing. This, no doubt, is because the traditional forms of education have been too limited in their objectives to serve the larger needs of our day.

Traditional education has aimed, first and foremost, at the individual's survival among his fellows. Such survival is indeed necessary, and when we write what follows we are casting no aspersions upon the schools but simply noting a fact.

What does the child study in the schools? First of all, reading, writing, and arithmetic—the so-called "tool" subjects. Why? To make the child a more broadly understanding individual? To develop his mind so that it will reach out over the world? He is taught reading, writing, and arithmetic in order that he may fit into a world where these things are indispensable. There are doubtless psychological effects which are by-products of these "tool" subjects—a certain orderliness and discipline of mind, a possibility of entrance into fascinating realms of reading; but primarily, the tool subjects serve the quite necessary function of providing the individual with the indispensable means for survival.

Let us pass from tool subjects to subjects like history and literature. What object do they serve? The answer, I think, is that where the tool subjects serve the purpose of individual survival, the cultural subjects chiefly serve the purpose of group survival. We frequently hear it said that the aim of education is to make good citizens. This, in other words, means that the aim is to develop individuals who will fit without friction into the cultural scheme. If we examine the history and literature that are taught, we find, in practically all cases, that they support the cultural scheme in which the child finds himself.

What this cultural scheme is can be noted by recalling

the three concepts which prevail, concepts which set the pattern for the child's thought and behavior.

The first of these is the concept of localism. Practically all the literature and history that have been available for teaching purposes have had the localistic note, the idea, namely, that humanity is inevitably divided into politically separated groups and that loyalty to one's group is the highest social virtue. We find it even in a philosopher like Plato. He wrote his ideal "Republic" on the pattern not of a world-state but of a little city with its enclosing walls and defending army.

The second concept that has prevailed has been the military one. This has followed logically from the localistic concept. In practically all literary and historical material available for use in the schools, it is taken for granted that groups will inevitably be at odds with one another and that the fundamental relationship between them is that of potential or actual enmity. I need hardly refer to the manner in which the military concept has been invested with such glamour as to make the virtue of martial heroism very nearly the high water mark of what is humanly desirable.

The third concept is somewhat difficult to describe. Let me first illustrate it. The child, let us say, reads a book of adventure. An explorer is killing a savage beast. The obvious feeling engendered in the child is one of pleasure in personal courage. And that, indeed, as far as it goes, is to the good. Or the child reads a romance in which an admirable young man has fallen in love with an equally admirable young woman. In this case, the obvious feeling engendered is one of pleasure in individual love. And that, too, as far as it goes, is to the good. Individual courage in the face of a foe and individual love for an individual beloved—these, perhaps, are the fine flower of what our children gather from literature.

But the adventure practically never goes beyond this meeting of specific dangers, the romance never beyond this absorption in a single beloved. This is not bad. But obviously it is not enough. For one can readily note that in such reading there is nothing that broadens the child's mind into a courage which faces the monsters that rear themselves against the world-weal—monsters like racial animosity, prejudice, mob-mindedness, social and political ignorance, war—nor into a love that embraces individuals of different race and class. As a matter of fact, children brought up on such literature of adventure and romance may, in the wider matters of human concern, remain as pathetically narrow, localistic, and even military-minded as those who are without its advantages.

How effectively, then, may a system of education make for the requisite social-mindedness which emphasizes, on the one hand, the tool subjects for personal survival, and, on the other, localism, militarism, and a narrowly restricted individualism?

There have, of course, been minds that placed a different emphasis upon matters and pointed the way to a more adequate culture. There was Kant, for example, with his *Essay on Perpetual Peace;* but Kant is hardly usable in the school room. And there was Spinoza, with his view of life that transcends the narrow bounds of sect and nation; but Spinoza, also, could hardly find his way into school textbooks. Above all, there was the Nazarene, with his universal viewpoint—of man as man, not as an American nor as a German, but as a son of God. But the Nazarene is not permitted, in the schools, to go counter to the strong cultural heritages of group aggressiveness and competitive individualism. He belongs to a Sunday school which fails to pass over into the Mondays and Tuesdays of secular education.

If the foregoing is true, it is clear what education, as we know it, actually does. American education is interested, primarily, in the perpetuation of American culture; it is not interested in exploring and perhaps adopting aspects of Hindu culture or Soviet culture. Nor, indeed, is it interested in a culture more adequate than any yet realized. It accepts American culture, and it takes it for granted that children are to be fitted into it, snugly and without friction.

It is therefore not difficult to realize why education has, in large measure, been a disappointment so far as the development of a more universalized mind is concerned. Education has deliberately aimed at perpetuating a view of life which, in essentials, either is indifferent or goes counter to world-understanding and wide social organization. If we realize this, we shall cease believing that when we place students in a classroom they will inevitably become social-minded. Unfortunately, they may remain just as narrow, localistic, and military-minded as ever.

THE MIND OF THE TEACHER

The first element of wisdom, I take it, is to realize that what we do in our schools, good as far as it goes, does not go so far as to build up the kind of minds required by our modern age. How are we now to take the further steps essential to a development of this type of mind?

We must begin with the teachers. As often as not, teachers, trained under a system which has laid stress on the ideas and objectives above mentioned, have, in their own attitudes, been a hindrance to the development of generous, outreaching, challenging attitudes on the part of the students. Teachers, for the most part, have served as effective exponents of the *status quo*. Something in their training has done this; something, too, in the authoritarian nature of the system in which they work has been responsible; something, also, in the relation expected of them to their community.

As to their teacher-training, it has centered chiefly upon methods of teaching. It has been in very small measure occupied with the fundamental problems of the world in which they live and are expected to work. Occupied with the best ways of teaching arithmetic, grammar, history, and the rest, prospective teachers have had their eyes turned away from the real perplexities and maladjustments of the social, political, and industrial world. Inevitably their teaching reflects their lack of concern with life as, in so great a measure, a difficult and fumbling effort to advance toward something more satisfyingly human.

What is needed, then, is the development of teachers who have a sense of the significance of evolution in human affairs. "The American college," writes President Morgan of Antioch—and the same might be said of the elementary schools—"should not merely sum up the prevailing culture and transmit it to the next generation. It should critically examine our civilization and contribute to its redesign and refinement. Our modern life halts in its progress, not only from inability to see clearly, but from a palsy of will and purpose and a lack of the spirit of adventure which leads men to undertake significant changes in the social order."

A teacher with a challenging mind would tend to produce students with challenging minds. But now we come to a second factor which stands in the way of the development of such minds. The schools are built on a pattern which largely discourages independence of thought and encourages passive agreement. The teacher is hired by a system, an authoritarian one. There are certain facts to be taught. These are rigidly prescribed. There is a monarch who surveys all that is taught, whose word is law and whose displeasure spells failure. And above the monarch is a super-monarch—a Board—whose word is the ultimate in authority. Schools, for the most part, are not delightful places where the teachers are a self-governing group of people with exploring minds trained to work in mutuality of spirit and in the expectation that they themselves, out of their own discussion and research, are to generate what is to be of value in the classroom. They are regimented to do a job, and the job is prescribed by rules.

The result is that all over the land teachers are notoriously timid in matters that go beyond the mere methodology of teaching. Having to fit into an authoritarian system, they tend to accept accepted things. They carry on the same old process of ushering acceptive minds into a world which, above all, needs minds with the power of discriminating challenge.

"Higher education," continues President Morgan—and again the same may be applied to the more elementary schools—"should be critical of remedies as well as of diseases—should lay sound foundations of knowledge and experience as a basis for social policies. When judgment is based upon sound scholarship and broad representative experience, it becomes a reasonably safe guide to vigorous action." Radicalism has a bad name because it is so frequently without a sound basis of critical judgment. But it is not radicalism that is to blame for this, but an educational system which, turning its face away from the controversial issues of social life, gives to young minds no training in critical social judgment.

There is also a third hindrance. We are proud of the fact—and rightly so—that education is deeply and integrally a community project. But when we find that the community, having done its best to secure trained people in whose care to place their children, listens in on the schoolroom teaching—whether in the person of Chambers of Commerce, military legions, or sons and daughters of this, that, and the other—and dictates what shall and what shall not be said and done, we have a situation that is educationally intolerable. It is as if the patient should say to the physician: "Cure me, but cure me according to my directions." This is what happens when local bodies, jealous, in their way, for the national or local weal, place their ban upon what the trained teachers may happen to teach. Nothing soundly reconstructive and critically progressive can take place in the schools and colleges until the public is educated to a policy of "hands off." By this I do not mean indifference. I mean a generous willingness to trust the trained persons it has chosen in the fields in which they have had their fundamental preparation.

Teachers with challenging minds, and a sense of the significance of evolution in human affairs; a school system democratic in spirit and organized for creative self-government; a public willing to keep interfering hands off—these, it would seem, are indispensable prerequisites if we are to advance to a type of education that even begins to generate minds adequate to the modern situation.

TOWARD WIDER RELATIONS

Given such teachers and such a school system, one might go far toward doing many things which now are not done. For example, there could be the tacit agreement that whatever was studied would, in some manner, be studied in its world context. History would lend itself immediately to such treatment. To enquire, while one was reading of the great days of Pericles, what was happening in what is now known as China, India, Russia, and the far-off British Isles, what was happening in Mexico and Peru, would give young people a vivid sense of the variety and the unity of the world process, would lead them to think always in terms that went beyond the particular locality and embraced the whole of mankind. What is really needed is to generate a new kind of emotion in people. Nations have been able to develop a strong emotion of love and admiration in their young people through the stories of their own particular struggles toward secure nationhood. We need now to pass to the next stage, to generate admiration and love for the fumbling, half-conscious effort of man everywhere to push life forward toward something more excellent. To have the student read history as the record of man's long struggle to win his emancipation from what is lower and less adequate is to help him to a new kind of affection for the mankind of which he and his nation are part.

Literature likewise lends itself to this universalizing treatment. Is it folk-tales that the child is reading? It would be illuminating to have him discover how the same tale is repeated all over the world. Is it a tale of heroism? He would find variations of it among most of the peoples of the world. Is it romance? It would be significant for him to learn when the finer forms of romance began to make their appearance among men and how widely they penetrate among the peoples of the world. Through such a study the student would unconsciously develop the habit of thinking of mankind as essentially one in nature and in destiny despite obvious differences of custom and organization.

Science, too, can be studied in its world context. The generous relations of scientists to one another, the carrying of the best that their minds have to offer across the boundaries of their local groups, the fine intelligence of man that has placed no customs' ban on the thoughts of the truthseekers, the widespread influence of scientific discoveries, the inter-knitting of peoples into a world-community of scientific give-and-take—all these things, made vivid, would go far to liberate students from narrow sectionalism and place them at the point of view of world coöperation in the search for understanding and control.

Thus we should stretch the minds of our students, give them wider areas in which to think, open up to them the possibilities of the whole human enterprise.

Again, with such teachers and such a system as we have described, there would inevitably be generated an attitude of pointing forward. These things—the fine flower of literature, the achievements of science, the struggles for liberty and order—are indeed great. But what can we now conceive as the greater that is to come? There is not a single study in which this forward-looking attitude cannot be in evidence. It requires only a vivid interest on the part of a teacher in the world as, in all its phases, an ongoing enterprise.

Finally, the essential wish of such teachers and of such a system would be to foster whatever is creative in the students. There would be little interest in developing a mere passive fulfillment of duties assigned. Discipline of mind and spirit would, indeed, be sought, but it would be sought as the outcome of personality awakened to interest and participation. The essential effort would be to stimulate independent thought and creative initiative, for it would be realized that the mind should be more than a machine that dutifully turns out what it is set to turn out. The human mind is itself the builder and director of machines and gains its dignity as it learns with fineness and surety of vision to create anew.

This is a spirit that is beginning to find its way even into the tradition-bound forms of our education. What is called "progressive education" in America, and the "new education" in England, is an attempt to compass these larger aims. Experiments in new types of college organization—notably those at Antioch, Swarthmore, Sarah Lawrence, and Bennington, and formerly at Wisconsin—have in one way and another been efforts to make education more truly a part of the ongoing enterprise of life. Not to impose patterns, but to train the builders of new patterns; not merely to adhere to the old standards, but to inspire students to find standards more adequate to our human undertaking—it is something of this nature that will increasingly animate the teachers of a more fortunate generation.

REMEMBERING THAT THERE ARE ADULTS

And now as to a matter that has been most sadly neglected. We have supposed education to be for children. Or at most for youths and maidens. Even here, however, our ideas have been changing, for gradually we have prolonged the years of childhood until, through high school and college, those years have advanced almost to maturity. But maturity is still neglected. It is a rare adult who deliberately carries on his education. But also, it is a rare community that gives him the opportunity to pursue the further cultivation of his mind.

There has hitherto been the assumption that everything which needs to be learned can be learned in childhood and youth. This, of course, is altogether untrue, for most of the problems that have to be confronted in adult life—those of household, politics, industry, child-rearing, mature sex life—can have no place in early education.

The next major insight of mankind will undoubtedly be that adulthood is just as deeply in need of education as childhood and youth, and that a community which makes no adequate provision for such education is simply working for its own stultification. It is the adult who faces most seriously the problems of human relations in a world of work and exchange, of competition and coöperation, of love and child-rearing. It is the adult who needs to know seriously what the whole human enterprise is about, what are the ways that lead to failure and the ways that lead to human triumph. Nothing very far-reaching can be achieved in the way of world-enlightenment or even of personal or group understanding until our civilization deliberately sets itself to the education of adults.

PURVEYORS OF ODDS AND ENDS

The carrying on of the enterprise of life requires a kind of wisdom of leadership. One would suppose that a richly equipped society would make more than ordinary efforts to develop leaders. It might be thought that those efforts are indeed being made. Are there not colleges and universities? Do not these, it might be asked, serve for the training of the superior minds and is not their training of the kind that makes for wise leadership?

Doubtless it once was so—to a degree; but the revolutions in industry and in the sciences through which we have passed have effected significant changes in these supposedly wisdom-developing institutions. Note the words: *uni*-versity and *col*-lege. Each, etymologically, gives the feeling of a drawing together of a diversity into a unity. In the early colleges and universities such a drawing together was in large measure achieved because of the focusing of all the studies upon a central interest. Whether the training was for the ministry or for the law, all the parts of it were intimately related and the individual came forth with a kind of totality of view, an integration or synthesis of understanding.

Much has happened since those simpler days to change this. With the expansion of the sciences into many hitherto unexplored fields and with the advance of economic enterprise, the older simplicities gave way before an increasing complexity. Science seemed to discover a magical secret—namely, that of dividing up the field of potential knowledge and setting each scientist assiduously to the tilling of his special acre. It was the parallel of the energetic individualism that ruled in the economic world. "Let each one pursue his specialty," the scientists seemed to say, "and all the specialties will somehow fall together into a common wisdom."

Would that it were so! We are just beginning to realize

that the optimism of economic *laissez faire* was misplaced. Where each individual pursued his own economic self-interest, it did not follow that an overruling providence wrought the various self-seekings into a social harmony. The confidence in scientific specialism begins similarly to be shaken. To learn the minutiae of some biological species does not of necessity guarantee broad scientific wisdom on the part of the researcher; nor does the mere adding of his increment of knowledge to all the other increments effect a sudden transformation of them all into an illuminating synthesis.

THE NEED OF PHILOSOPHY

It is significant that we call this the Age of Science. We do not call it the Age of Philosophy. Philosophy is a seeking after wisdom, and wisdom, as we have seen, is a judgment made in the light of some kind of integration of parts. Perhaps it is toward an Age of Philosophy that we are now moving, for there has seldom been so widespread a call for the correlation of our efforts, for the bringing of plan into our unplanned social enterprises, for the setting of some kind of acceptable goal for all our economic, political, scientific, and social endeavors.

However, insistent though the call may be for this more comprehensive type of thinking, the failure to achieve it is the disappointing fact. Economists cannot seem to pass beyond the details of economic processes to comprehensive human considerations. More particularly, they cannot seem to pass beyond symptoms to causes, but persist in offering their specialized palliatives in the face of a movement of life that is sweeping away old practices and institutions. Politicians battle over sales-taxes, budget-balancings, and small measures of relief, apparently unable to comprehend the fact that it is the movement toward a new civilization that should have their attention. Business men look for an uprise in this or that industry, hailing some new invention with an almost devotional ardor in a hope that it may be the means to unlock fresh purchasing power. And ordinary people call for bonuses, or farm-relief, or loans to the indigent.

All this is not surprising. We lack comprehensive minds because the instrumentalities of education have not been directed toward the development of such minds. Education has followed the lead of science and technology and has become an enterprise in specialties. Almost as soon as a child is led from the sandpile to his first book, he begins to be bombarded with uncorrelated facts. Facts multiply as he passes through the grades. By the time he reaches high school, he is in a rush from one set of facts to another —in algebra, literature, biology, chemistry, and so on. When he enters college, the situation continues unaltered. The world has come to be so full of a number of things that colleges and universities have felt called upon to introduce very nearly every possible subject into the curriculum, so that a college student, required to do his duty by the vast miscellany, spends his years in a kind of breathless dash from one area of hastily surveyed facts to another.

"The net result of all this is that our conception of

general education has become a collection of odds and ends for which it is impossible to have any profound respect. . . .

"In view of this development, it is no wonder that there has been increasing dissatisfaction with the college of liberal arts. Its original unity of purpose has been completely lost. This fact can scarcely be disguised by vague talk about the breadth or background to be obtained from a college education. The vaunted breadth is not so much breadth as a confusion of breadth with variety. We have incorporated a number of diverse values into the curriculum by a process of compartmentalization. We teach a little of everything, and then we apparently expect the students to achieve out of the total mass of their learnings a synthesis which, up to the present, the college has been quite unable to achieve for itself.

"This is bad enough, but it does not tell the whole story. The compartmentalization . . . becomes a means for concealing from the student the things that he is most in need of knowing, if he is to lead an intelligent life. The compartmental divisions tend to obscure the fact that these various values or interests are in serious conflict with one another. Traditional religion and traditional culture, for example, have never harmonized well. The one has its center in a realm beyond the skies; the other in a domain that does not pretend to be anything but a product of the human mind. . . . Our traditional conceptions of conduct and personal development are hopelessly out of tune with modern industry and business, where the law of the jungle still holds sway. The students, like the college itself, have inherited all these discordant elements, and no concerted effort is made to set them straight. They come in adhering to all these diverse standards, and they go out in essentially the same condition. They have secured no basis for intelligent living. The various elements in their education tend to neutralize one another, and so the final result is apathy or intellectual and emotional paralysis." [1]

NEW GOVERNORS FOR OLD

Another factor has entered to make the situation worse. In the earlier years of colleges and universities, the governing boards were largely composed of clergymen. We have a way now of being scornful of gentlemen of the cloth and of congratulating ourselves that the rule of dogmatic piety is over. But it is a question whether in departing from the older type of college government, we have bettered our lot. Clergymen at least had a view of life that possessed a certain comprehensiveness. Despite frequent flaws in their thinking, they had a fair notion of what life was about and how it should be lived. In their government of colleges and universities, therefore, they stressed the unities and the fundamental human values.

During the past few decades, the government of higher education has fallen into new hands—those of lawyers and men of business. Neither art, science, literature, housewifery, nor labor have in due proportion been represented

[1] *Aims in College Teaching*, by Boyd H. Bode. Bulletin of the American Association of University Professors, page 26. January, 1933.

on these governing boards. Since lawyers are increasingly the aides of business enterprise, we may say that the government of higher education has passed into the hands of business. The consequence is that the objectives of business have made themselves strongly felt in colleges and universities.

In the first place, there has been an increasing emphasis upon size. Big buildings, big classrooms, big student bodies, big contributions, big output. In the second place, there has been an increasing emphasis upon multiplication of courses. The aim of business is to produce in order to sell. Colleges and universities exist in order to sell their various wares. Thus governing bodies have encouraged the adding of courses with a kind of indiscriminate lavishness, until a college curriculum is as multitudinous—and as uncorrelated—as a Sears Roebuck catalogue.

It is most astonishing that it should ever have occurred to anyone that the policies of higher education could properly be directed by men of business. The explanation, indeed, might be that, in a young country, colleges and universities need financial support and that business men are the experts who can best secure the requisite support. What has actually occurred has been that the financial governors have served not only as experts of finance but as guardians of basic policy. Business men are enterprisers in the *status quo*. They are peculiarly sensitive to anything that disturbs the processes whereby they carry on their operations. Hence they have brought an increasing pressure to bear to keep colleges and universities "safe," with the result that the spirit of independent research in all matters effecting economic and political life has been more or less openly discouraged.

As Charles Beard has written: "For government by the fellowship of scholars was substituted government by a board of trustees and a president. The trustees were united by no common bond of identical intellectual discipline. They gave little or no attention to the educational side of management (for which the institution was supposed to exist), except when there was trouble, when some professor said or did something out of the ordinary which shocked friends, founders, and benefactors. The president acted as a kind of buffer. He was seldom a dictator, for, whatever his personal desires, he usually found himself hemmed in on all sides by the pressures of special interests in the faculty and the board of trustees. Thus it happened that chaos presided over chaos. The powers of order were brought to bear only when there was some unusual disturbance—when a professor expressed doubts about the intellectual advantages of military training or the beneficence of British rule in India. In such circumstances the professor . . . became a kind of hired man to be fired without notice by his employers—the president and trustees—if he said anything extraordinary, either wise or foolish. Safety, then, lay in a still more extreme specialization or in using the patois of the lowest common denominator in the community. For the seeker after truth to discover anything not known to the village clergyman or the man in the street became perilous. . . .

"There seemed to be no way to resolve the antithesis.

If the corporate financiers and managers were right, then it was the business of the professor to stick to his last and obey orders or take his walking papers without any question. If the professors were right, if the university existed for scholarship and the advancement of learning, as announced on various ceremonial occasions, then surely the scholars and teachers immersed in learning ought to form the governing fellowship and to act as judges whenever one of their number transgressed the bounds of propriety. . . .

"Something significant would doubtless happen if those on the opposite sides of the barbed-wire entanglement would ask themselves, sincerely, honestly, and under the eye of eternity: 'What, after all, is the supreme duty of intelligence and the ultimate function of the university in the universe?' It would be interesting to catch a few university presidents off guard, a few deans disengaged from registration cards, and a few professors not busy with splitting hairs already split a thousand times, and to hurl this *elenchus* into their midst. Some would laugh, no doubt, others would suddenly remember that they had a luncheon engagement, still others would think it 'academic.' But until it is asked with the kind of insistence which an Eliot or a Gilman could employ, it is not probable that anything really significant will take place in the American world of higher learning." [2]

As the challenge of a new day confronts us, we are beginning to recognize that this purveying of a mental mis-

[2] *The Quest for Academic Power*, by Charles A. Beard. Bulletin of the American Association of University Professors, page 18. January, 1933.

cellaneity, under the direction of business men who have conspicuously failed to build a noble civilization and of professors who have retreated into the safe areas of their specialties, is not education in the true sense of the word. Above all it is not the kind of education that can produce the leadership necessary in our complicated new world.

CONCLUSION

And so we confront the necessity of re-surveying our educational aims and practices. Not all education is good because it goes by that name. It is necessary now for us to ask what we really wish our schools and colleges to do. Do we wish them to develop individuals trained to the traditional acceptances, each individual expert in his own limited area, each prepared to perpetuate a world that was "good enough for our fathers"? Or do we wish them to develop individuals capable of looking forward and of moving forward into ways of life more in keeping with our emerging conceptions? If it is the second that we wish, then our educational system must be subjected to a thoroughgoing examination of its methods and objectives.

What we shall be as a civilization will depend largely upon what we train our people to be. Hence the problem of bringing education into conformity with our developing ideas is perhaps as vital as any that we face.

CHAPTER 8. THE FIVE-FOLD WISDOM

THERE are five wisdoms which education will doubtless attempt to achieve for young and old.

There is first of all a wisdom of the body. The body is our primary instrument. Awkward, or clogged with poisons, or overmastered by timidities or passions, it serves poorly. Obviously the first of the life-wisdoms is to make it into as perfect an instrument as we possibly can.

Browning no doubt had in mind such a joyous wisdom of the body when he had the young David sing:

"Oh, our manhood's prime vigour! no spirit feels waste,
Not a muscle is stopped in its playing, nor sinew unbraced.
Oh, the wild joys of living! the leaping from rock up to rock—
The strong rending of boughs from the fir-tree,—the cool silver shock
Of the plunge in a pool's living water, . . .
How good is man's life, the mere living! how fit to employ
All the heart and the soul and the senses, for ever in joy!" [1]

We begin to attend to bodily wisdom in the home. Diet, fresh air, sleep, habit-formation—all these are the concern

[1] Robert Browning, *Saul.*

of wise parents. It begins now to be the concern of the more alert schools and colleges, where wholesome surroundings, sunlight and fresh air, recreation, well-cooked food have been substituted for the screwed-down seats, the airless rooms, the military regimentation, and the clammy cold lunches of the older days. Education begins to be aware that it is as seriously concerned with the building up of wholesome bodies as it is with the building up of educated minds.

But much still remains unaccomplished. "Shades of the prison house begin to close" upon the growing child. Even in the best schools, adolescence is still recognized as little more than a passing phase in the life of children, to be accorded no special attention. The psychology of adolescence is, indeed, duly studied by teachers, and it is taken for granted that peculiar emotional upsets are apt to occur in that period. But at this stage when young life craves release from cramping conditions, when it is all set for various adventure, the best that is offered is the opportunity for entrance into high-pressure athletics. Little or no effort is made to train for grace, suppleness, and resourcefulness in the hobble-de-hoy bodies—such training as can be had in long hikes, in horseback-riding, in camping, in spontaneous dramatics, and in those games that enlist not only all the muscles of the body but the mind as well. Instead, the adolescent in the high school is chained to a multitude of books which to him are fairly meaningless, until a frustrated mind is generated in a largely frustrated body. For it can hardly be said that the brief excursions into gymnastic exercises or athletics are all that the body at this period of life craves and needs. Physical training is usually as highly specialized and out of correlation with all the other activities of life as everything else in education is, and, as often as not, in the hands of teachers unaware of the wholeness of the life they are training, it becomes either a negligible but boresome requirement, or a positive detriment.

It is significant of practically all that we do with the physical life that we stress only the aspect of muscular health. We pay practically no attention to the body as an instrument of ideas and emotions. Thus the prize athlete of the school may seem awkward and constrained as he stands up to try to express himself, or as he walks in and out of a room. An intelligent woman—formerly an actress—who works in a spontaneous kind of dramatics with children, suggests to her youngsters, "See if you can make your body say this," and with an exquisite kind of rightness they make their bodies *speak*.

It is in adult life particularly that we note the failure of the school to train a kind of wisdom of the body. Adults are all too frequently graceless in their standing and sitting, in their goings forth and comings in. For the most part, their voices are not instruments of beauty. Their bodies seem inconsequential appendages of their minds, playing no part in expressiveness. Indeed, their arms and legs seem to serve only as a kind of tool for moving things—and themselves—from one spot in space to another.

To develop the body as a beautiful and resourceful instrument of the inner life—that might be an objective worth pursuing in our schools and colleges.

A SECOND WISDOM

There is a second wisdom—wisdom in human relations. Not much can be expected of schools and colleges that are content to organize themselves on the competitive pattern that rules in a world of ugly economic relationships. The first need of a truly emancipated education will be to renounce the world and the devil and to claim the right to develop among its students and teachers human relationships that have some degree of loveliness. Thus, there is no place in education for the pedagogical tyrant, ruling with terrifying authority from a platform. How many of us have encountered that kind of educational monstrosity, usually a timid and mediocre creature gaining an easy superiority over defenseless youngsters—an educational replica of the managerial bully or the financial exploiter. Nor will there be any place in education for that competitive process of each for himself where reciting becomes a process of cleverly accommodating oneself to the idiosyncrasies of the teacher and of fashioning one's ignorances into an appearance of acceptable knowledge. Most of the evils which bulk large in the adult world have their preliminary tryouts in the bluffing, cheating, pandering, and sharp-eyed seeking for the main chance which are bred in school rooms that "prepare children for life."

The schools and colleges must come to know that it is not their task to prepare young people for the kind of life that now largely exists in the adult world, but rather to utilize the time at their command for developing more generous human relationships. The most important of these will be the working-together relationship. The schools and colleges have done much to develop a fine playing-together relationship. Good sportsmanship is perhaps the most precious ethical quality that has come out of modern education. There needs also to be developed a kind of good sportsmanship in working-together, the spirit of generous contribution, of recognition of the contributions of others, and that spirit which cares more about the success of the joint enterprise than about individual distinction.

Education has the real opportunity of giving young people a taste of what a generously coöperative life can be. If when young people emerge from the school room, they are shocked by the far different spirit which rules among harassed and self-seeking adults, the shock may be a salutary one. It will at least prevent them from too easily carrying on the old unlovelinesses.

A THIRD

There is a third necessary wisdom—that of appreciation. Man's history has been a long fumbling forward out of savagery into some kind of civilized existence. During that long fumbling he has made many a tragic mistake which has thrown him back or prevented his onward movement. But he has also had his moments of triumph. In the dim beginnings of history, a Ptah Hotep speaks of the courtesies, of justice, and of friendship; a Lao Tze meditates upon the boundlessness that encompasses the petty details of life; a Socrates stands on the street corner conversing of wisdom and straightness of thinking; a Euripides puts words of a new kind of compassion into the mouths of his actors; a Jesus talks to the multitudes by a lakeside; a Galileo shapes a crude telescope and sweeps a universe within his vision; a Leonardo paints a Last Supper; a Beethoven writes an "Eroica"; a Shelley sings of skylarks and a Promethean self. . . .

To grasp something of the heroism of man's struggle beyond animalhood is, in a sense, to make oneself part of that struggle.

"Sunset and silence! A man; around him earth savage, earth broken;
Beside him two horses, a plough!

Earth savage, earth broken, the brutes, the dawn-man there in the sunset,
And the plough that is twin to the sword, that is founder of cities! . . .

Slowly the darkness falls, the broken lands blend with the savage;
The brute-tamer stands by the brutes, a head's breadth only above them.

A head's breadth? Ay, but therein is hell's depth and the height up to heaven,
And the thrones of the gods and their halls, their chariots, purples, and splendours." [2]

[2] Padraic Colum, from *The Plougher;* from *Wild Earth and Other Poems;* by permission of The Macmillan Company, publishers.

To live greatly in one's world, one must companion with man's greater triumphs. For in them undoubtedly lies most of what is authentic and fruitful in humanity.

A FOURTH

Then there is work. Work, we now know, is no curse—unless, in our stupidity or our cruelty, we make it so.

"*You work that you may keep pace with the earth and the soul of the earth.*

"*For to be idle is to become a stranger unto the seasons, and to step out of life's procession, that marches in majesty and proud submission towards the infinite. . . .*

"*Always you have been told that work is a curse and labour a misfortune.*

"*But I say to you that when you work you fulfil a part of earth's furthest dream, assigned to you when that dream was born,*

"*And in keeping yourself with labour you are in truth loving life,*

"*And to love life through labour is to be intimate with life's inmost secret.*" [3]

[3] Kahlil Gibran, from *The Prophet;* by permission of Alfred A. Knopf, publisher.

One of the outstanding failures of education is that it has turned its face away from the work-life. It has permitted that life to be ruled in the spirit of ruthlessness and unconcern for human value. Schools and colleges have operated in the midst of the incredible work-slaveries of our manufacturing cities and have neither uttered protest nor trained their students for a more acceptable life. In this, as in other things, schools and colleges have shown themselves to be the timid acceptors of a *status quo*, rather than the prophets of a civilization more nearly related to genuine human values. It is of course the privilege of these institutions to serve lower values if that is what they feel they must do. But the sensitive educator must rest uneasy as he contemplates the havoc which an industrialized civilization has wrought of the enduring need of man to find for himself a work that is at once a contribution and a self-release.

Education, therefore, must lend itself to discovering the wisdom of vocation: that wisdom, namely, which enables the individual to marshal his energies in furtherance of that which is both a delight to himself and a value for his society.

A FIFTH

Finally there must be a wisdom as to life-objectives. Young people must be helped to find out for themselves what the life-enterprise is about. For the most part, they are permitted to drift into adulthood with no clear notion as to their own part or even of society's part in the furtherance of human values. As frequently as not, they have no thought of any values save those that contribute to their own success. They are not to be blamed for this. They pass through a secular schooling which instructs them in particularities, but which leaves these particularities hanging loose and unsynthesized. Thus they gain no sense of the meaning of social enterprises, nor of the significant part which they themselves can play in them. Again, they pass—if they do—through a religious training which speaks a language so impractically idealistic that it fails to carry over into daily behavior.

The story is told of Bishop Grundtvig, the great Danish educator, that when he gathered his groups of young adults together, he did not teach them facts out of books. He talked with them informally of history—of what it signified, of the long struggle of man to win his way to civilization; he discussed with them particularly the history of their own land, trying to discover what it was that the life of Denmark really meant and could mean to its people and to the world. He discussed the works of poets, musicians, artists, scientists and inventors, until his young people grasped something of the noble directions that life could take. The influence of Grundtvig was very great, developing as it did into a movement of education that regenerated Denmark, because Grundtvig's point of view was that of the philosopher. Always his effort was to see life whole, to see it in its meaning and in its great ways of functioning. The men who went forth from his teaching sixty odd years ago carried with them a vision that enabled them to go forward with single-minded confidence in the upbuilding of their then depressed and demoralized land.

It is something of this spirit of the philosopher that is needed in our education. We are at present lost in the very riches of our civilization's achievements. We give our students practically no sense of vital relationships. In an age that boasts of air-mindedness, we provide little opportunity for young minds to make their flights above the bewildering jungle of specialties and to sense the lay of the human land. Education of the future will seek for the wisdom that embraces all the manifold details of life in a comprehensive grasp of what life is for. It will cease, in short, to be a mere transmitter of a factual and cultural miscellany and be an integrator of all that is valid into a unity of vision and of high desire.

CONCLUSION

It is this five-fold way of wisdom—of the body, of human relations, of appreciation, of vocation, and of life-objectives—that is the authentic way of education. When that way is taken, all the fact-learnings and the tool-learnings will fall into their proper places. They will be found to be incidental to the major processes of learning to be wise. When the schools and colleges can help individuals to be greatly wise, they will at last be training the leaders for the civilization that is to be.

CHAPTER 9. A MAJOR SCIENCE IN NEED OF REVISION

THE science of economics, as it has been developed during the past few decades, has been incapable of making a broadly human valuation of the processes with which it deals. Not only has it been incapable; it has frankly made no pretense to the undertaking. This is doubtless the more surprising to the lay reader, who, recognizing the commanding place held in life by economic problems, is led to believe that a valuation of them in terms of human welfare is wholly necessary. The modern economist, however, has been perfectly clear about his position. He has regarded his work as descriptive, not evaluative.

Moreover, in pursuance of his purely descriptive endeavor, the economist has carefully divested certain basic concepts which he has employed of the usual evaluative connotations. These are the concepts of utility, cost, and value. As ordinarily conceived, utility connotes usefulness, adaptation to an end which makes for human welfare. Whiskey, for example, has utility when it revives a stricken man; it can scarcely be said to have utility when it plunges a man into sodden drunkenness. A stick of dynamite has utility when it blasts rocks; it can scarcely be said to have utility when it is used to blow up a houseful of innocent people. In the broad human meaning of the term, in short, utility attaches to all those things and relations that stand on the credit side of human welfare.

On the other hand, from the same human point of view, cost attaches to all those things and relations that stand on the debit side of human welfare. Excessive toil, for example, involves so much of cost to the muscular and nervous system; overeating and drinking involve so much of cost to the digestive organs.

Nothing is more necessary to an understanding of the scope of economics and its bearing upon our human issues than the realization that the meanings above outlined are not those which economists for the most part have assigned when they have used these apparently evaluative terms. "The utility of a thing to a person at a time," said Marshall,[1] "is measured by the extent to which it satisfies his wants. And wants are here reckoned quantitatively, that is, with regard to their volume and intensity; they are not reckoned qualitatively according to any ethical or prudential standard." From the economic point of view, in short, as against the ordinary human point of view, the whiskey has just as legitimate a claim to utility when it serves to induce drunkenness as when it serves medical purposes. What determines economic utility, in brief, is the power to satisfy some human want. The want may be good or bad for the individual or society. This, though of consequence to us as human beings, is of no consequence to the economist. "These qualities in economic goods which satisfy

[1] *Principles of Economics*, Vol. I; page 167.

human wants . . . must not be confounded with usefulness; for it is perfectly possible for a commodity to possess utility without being useful. A diamond pin may not be useful, but it may satisfy one's desire for show. In economics the word *utility* signifies the presence of some want-satisfying quality." [2] In the determination of utility the individual consumer is the final judge. "The fact that the consumer is willing to give up something in order to procure an article proves once and for all that for him it has utility—it fills a want." [3]

It follows that all consumable or usable commodities, all commodities, in fact, for which there is in any sense a demand, are utilities. From which it likewise follows that according to traditional economic understanding, disutility does not exist in the realm of commodities.

On the other hand, disutility, or cost, has been assigned to all those processes which are required for the satisfaction of wants. The labor expended in producing or in manufacturing the goods which satisfy wants has been understood by the economist to be the exact antithesis of a utility: it has in every sense and in all cases been "cost." "The exertions," says Marshall,[4] "of all the different kinds of labor that are directly or indirectly involved in making the commodity; together with the abstinences or rather the waitings required for saving the capital used in making it: all these efforts and sacrifices together will be called the *real cost of production* of the commodity."

[2] Burch and Nearing, *Elements of Economics,* page 24.
[3] Taussig, *Principles of Economics,* Vol. I; page 120.
[4] *Principles of Economics,* Vol. I; page 148.

There has been no thought that expenditure of effort may involve utility even to the one who makes the effort, as, for example, in the case of the artist; or that sacrifice or waiting may have utility to him who sacrifices or waits, as in the development of forethought and self-control. According to the economist's meaning all sacrifices whether of labor or time have been counted equally as costs.

THE ECONOMIC AND THE HUMAN POINT OF VIEW

We note, thus, a very pronounced contrast between the economic and the human understanding of these basic concepts. According to the traditional economist all goods (commodities) are utilities; all efforts are costs. According to the ordinary human point of view not all goods are utilities; and not all efforts are costs: some economic costs have no human costs attached to them; while some economic utilities involve decided human costs.

The divergence of economic analysis from human valuation has been exhibited most sharply, however, in the contrast between the economic and the human meaning of "value." According to Seager, value has two meanings in economics, subjective and objective. In the subjective meaning value is "the importance which a person ascribes to a unit of good as a condition to the gratification of his wants." The objective meaning of value is value in exchange, "the power of a good to command other goods in exchange for itself." As the second is the meaning almost wholly in use in economic science, little attention is given to the first. Value in exchange is measured by dollars and cents. A book costs a dollar; a burglar's jimmy costs a dollar. From the point of view of economic value—value in exchange—they are equal, for each "good" has precisely the same power which the other has to "command other goods in exchange for itself."

"It is no concern of ours to criticise this attitude in the sense of condemnation. But it is important to realize that no progress of psychological analysis will enable economic science to supply a human valuation of industry so long as all human functions involved in economic processes are measured, assessed and valued according to their bearing upon the production of a 'wealth' which has no directly assignable relation to human welfare, but is estimated by a purely monetary measure." [5]

The current belief that economics is the last word in the evaluation of economic processes and relationships is a profound and misleading error, one for which the more accurate economists are themselves not to blame. Economics, as traditionally developed, is at best only a description of the technique of narrowly pecuniary processes. It is in no sense a broadly human evaluation of those processes.

BROADENING THE CONCEPT OF WORK

A good number of years ago, Mr. J. A. Hobson, the distinguished English economist, in the book above mentioned, made a critical distinction between the abstractly limited conceptions of the then regnant economics and the

[5] Hobson, J. A., *Work and Wealth: A Human Valuation,* page 8. By permission of The Macmillan Company, publishers.

broader conceptions which an economics applicable to human affairs would seem to require. The critical analysis which he then made is now so timely that I am venturing to outline it in the following pages.

A human evaluation of economic goods and processes would, he showed, in contrast with the conventional one, define "utility" as that which supports or adds to human welfare; "cost" as that which undermines or subtracts from human welfare; "value" as the ultimate balance of utility and cost from the point of view of the best ordering of human life.

When we apply such interpretations of utility, cost, and value to the processes of production, distribution, and consumption, we note the significant fact that not all goods are utilities and not all efforts are costs. Cost, in brief, belongs as properly as utility upon the side of consumptive enjoyment; while utility belongs as properly as cost on the side of productive effort. This, of course, turns the ordinary economics upside down.

It is obvious, for example, that not all efforts of labor count as so much to the human bad. The creative work of the artist, for example, even though it involves a stern discipline and weary labor, is a joy. It is more to the artist than the goods which he consumes. Indeed in many cases the act of creating is far more fascinating than the contemplation of the finished product. Here, then, is a type of labor which is in large measure costless.

Slightly below the wholly creative artist in the pure fascination of their work are the scientist and the scholar. In the case of these, creative imagination must be harnessed to fact. The pursuit of fact involves many elements of routine, monotony, patience, perseverance. The work, in short, is not all costless. And yet so far do the scientific and scholarly interests outweigh the wearisome labors, that the cost aspect of such labors is but slight. Here again, there is frequently as much satisfaction of wants in the actual process of working as in the contemplation of the achieved results. Achievement is but the stimulus and the invitation to the joys of further work.

Below the artist and scientist are those who partake of their spirit, yet who fail of their genius: on the one hand the art interpreters—actors, musicians, critics, readers; on the other hand, the teachers of science and scholarship. There is still a large measure of joy in the work of these who stand thus but a little lower, so large a measure that most of them prefer this nearness to the creative genius of life even at the cost of smaller rewards. The teacher puts up, not always gladly, yet resignedly enough, with a limited income; the actor would not forego his economically precarious commerce with his gods for the fattest income of the financier. The creative spark may be but feeble but it is alight in these ranks; and here again the light is its own reward. The work of these lower ones is full of cost—toilsome travel, insecure tenures, wearisome learning of lines; or the reading of examination papers, the organization of grades, the attendance upon administrative duties. But, with it all, the fascination outweighs the toilsomeness; and the work shows a clear balance on the side of utility as over against cost.

On practically the same level as the interpreters are the

professional men—physicians, lawyers, engineers, architects. The labor of such workers is indeed full of cost—wear and tear of nervous and muscular energy, the exclusion from free creative work, the subordination of personal interests to the needs of patients and clients. But, on the whole, for all the heavy cost involved, there remains a large measure of professional labor that is humanly costless, that stimulates and fascinates and brings happiness.

To enter into all the niceties of an analysis such as the foregoing paragraphs suggest would carry us to a length beyond the purpose of the present chapter. It remains but to advert to the two types of effort that are perhaps most widely in evidence—those of the organizer-manager and of the routine worker. In the case of the former, the work, at its high level, may in quality approach very nearly to that both of the creative artist and the scientist. It possesses the fascination that resides in the investigation and the constructive assembling of powers and interests. Thus the great financier is not only a close student of subtle economic relationships; he is likewise an organizer of them into new forms and to new ends. But with this creative activity, in itself costless, there goes the nervous cost of excitement and uncertainty. Great fortunes are made and unmade. A turn of the market may plunge a man to ruin. A failure of crops or a social disturbance may wreck plans elaborated with consummate genius. A constant watchfulness, an unremitting concern with the niceties of economic relations tie a man night and day, in season and out of season, to "business." He tends to sacrifice broader interests, to lose a wider flexibility of mind. "Probably the heaviest human cost, however, is a certain moral callousness and recklessness involved in the financial struggle. For the paper symbols of industrial power, which financiers handle, are so abstract in nature and so remote from the human facts which they direct, that the chain of causation linking stocks and shares with human work and human life is seldom realized."[6]

As we descend from the creative work of the financier to the more conventional and routine work of business organization, we find an increase in cost through the diminution of the creative factor and the increase of the factor of laborious routine. In many instances, however, this increase in human cost is in large measure counterbalanced by a diminution of the cost which the financier suffers by reason of his aloofness from the human factor in industry. The smaller entrepreneur is nearer to working men and women and is for that reason less liable to the deadening or the perversion of his human understanding and sympathy.

When we pass from the managerial plane of effort to that of routine labor, we find, as we are now doubtless prepared to expect, a very large increase in human cost. In one sense, indeed, the laborer is freed from that type of cost which is peculiar to the managerial class—the risks of enterprise; but obviously this freedom is more than counterbalanced by the more pressing and imminent risk of destitution. The anxiety of the financier has in it an element of sportsman's hazard; the anxiety of the routine worker has in it little save the fear of the hunted creature.

[6] Hobson, *op. cit.*, page 56.

But the heaviest costs of routine labor lie in the four factors of fatigue, monotony, lack of interest, and dependence. Fatigue, we now know, has actual toxic effects upon the physiological structure. Monotony dulls the mind and devitalizes the body, awakening an abnormal craving for stimulants to prod the jaded organism. Lack of vital interest in the work keeps the worker entirely outside his labor, which, consequently, is not invested with dignity in his own eyes. Labor for him is a means to something other than itself—to the money that it brings. Unlike the creative artist, his work is his sacrifice and his degradation, not his glory. Finally, complete dependence upon the will of others who direct, divests him of essential claims to respect. He is either weakly resigned or sullenly but impotently rebellious.

AN EVALUATION OF INTEREST

It is in this manner that Mr. Hobson indicated the type of analysis which must be made if the "effort" factor in economic processes is to be humanly measured. To lump all types of effort together as costs, he felt, was simply to ignore vital distinctions—distinctions that must be grasped if we are to attain to a clear understanding of the relation of work, on the one hand, to economic reward, and on the other, to human welfare.

There is another covering-up of vital distinctions that he felt should be noted. According to the traditional economist there is a second type of effort that must figure wholly on the cost side of the economic balance sheet, "the abstinences or rather waitings required for saving . . . capital." If abstinence and waiting are indeed costs, there would seem to be entire propriety, moral as well as economic, in compensating by economic reward. The institution of interest, apparently, is the social recognition of this fact.

Are the abstinence and waiting, however, involved in the act of saving always to be counted as human costs? An analysis of the situation, according to Hobson, reveals four types of savers: the rich, who save automatically; the middle class who fall into two groups, those who save as a matter of forethought and self-control, and those who are induced to save by the lure of interest; and the poor, who save with difficulty and sacrifice.

In the saving of the rich, there is involved no actual abstinence or waiting. It is obvious, therefore, that no human cost attaches to such saving; and any economic compensation given to counter-balance the supposed cost is so much social waste. As to those of the middle class who save as a matter of forethought and self-control, saving is simply a means of making a more advantageous outlay of income, spreading its use, that is, over a number of years, instead of consuming it immediately, and providing for the non-earning future. Saving in this sense is to the advantage of the saver; and again, in so far, involves no real human costs. It would be effected whether interest were offered or not.

A more difficult situation presents itself with regard to those of the middle class who save only by reason of the stimulus of interest—the naturally thoughtless and extravagant folk. For such folk to save implies an actual effort of abstinence which may at times amount to the real pain of deprivation. Is this effort a human cost? Obviously the real cost here is the human recklessness and lack of forethought. If interest is paid, it is paid not as compensation for an actual human cost, but as a bait to lure persons away from a type of indulgence which is itself actual cost.

In all these cases, then, according to Hobson, interest is not, properly speaking, a compensation for cost. In the first two cases it is socially needless and wasteful; in the third case (involving, as a matter of fact, only a relatively small portion of society) it is at best a doubtful lure to forethought and self-control. The fourth case, however, is strikingly different. The poor person who saves often does so at the cost of life necessities. A family will deny itself nourishing cuts of meat, proper clothing, sufficient fuel, in order to put aside the little weekly amount in the bank. Or it may curtail its recreational and cultural life—it may give up vacations; it may take the children earlier from school. All these are fundamental human costs. If interest is paid, it is here indeed paid for costs. But here, where alone interest is a payment for human costs, it is a stimulus to persons to suffer costs which as a matter of fact they ought not to be required to suffer.

It is obvious, then, how a human as against a purely economic analysis of abstinence and waiting discloses factors in the situation which awaken significant reflections upon one of the most approved economic practices—the payment of interest. Other factors in the situation—risk, stimulation of enterprise, et cetera—would have to be discussed before a careful conclusion could be reached as to the proper place of interest in an economy. What Hobson was especially concerned to make clear is the thought that the factors—abstinence and waiting—which traditional economic science ranges without discrimination wholly on the cost side of the *economic* ledger belong as a matter of fact in large measure on the opposite side of the *human* ledger.

TYPES OF CONSUMPTION

The foregoing exposition of Hobson's method of human analysis of economic processes enables us to indicate with comparative brevity how he would attack the remaining basic issues of economic life.

Over against the processes of production are those of consumption. Economic science places these altogether on the utility side of the balance sheet. Shall we accept this as also the judgment of a human valuation; or shall we find that here, too, as in the case of productive effort, the human values differ from what they would seem to be when the considerations are wholly economic?

Three factors are present as determinants of the consumption process: organic needs, commercial pressure, social prestige. The organic needs of bodily and mental growth and vigor are strong enough to call into being a mass of goods whose relation to life is altogether one of utility. The staple foods and textiles, wood, iron, and steel for shelter and transportation, coal, oil, gas, electricity for fuel and light, books containing information about the life processes—all these are essential to any effective ordering of life; but it is obvious at once that the factors of commercial pressure and social prestige enter to confuse and misdirect the organic issues of life. Where the aim of the manufacturer is not serviceableness, but profit, various interferences with the organic needs disclose themselves. Adulteration and deceptive imitation work greater or less harm. All such commodities then must, in proportion to their harmfulness, be placed on the side of cost. But the manufacturer and the vender of commodities may also, through various subtle devices of appeal, stimulate cravings that are not only low, but distinctly injurious. Such, for example, are the stimulations of the burlesque house, sensuous music, lurid newspapers. The commercial enterprise has an enormous advantage over the consumer in so far as, with single eye to profit, it can organize wide and persistent campaigns of subtle stimulation which rouse in the unsuspecting and unorganized consumers desires and cravings which would otherwise scarcely have been felt. In this campaign of subtle stimulation an almost incalculable number of commodities are produced—posters, placards, pamphlets, pictures, cartoons, newspaper advertisements—not to speak of the actual articles which these are intended to sell—which are distinctly injurious in their end-results. Thus there is a proportion of goods which, instead of standing, as the economist in his purely neutral account indicates, on the credit side of the human balance, stands unquestionably on the debit side.

But another factor not so commonly recognized plays a large part in diverting production and consumption from organic channels. The craving to be distinguished from one's fellows is doubtless as old as human nature. In primitive society this craving realized itself through exploit; the doer of big things, either in the hunt or war, was the great man. A new means of securing distinction is necessary for a civilization of peace. Two principles of distinction have developed, one valuable, the other valueless. Distinction through service—of scholarship, science, art, statesmanship—is for many persons the only type of distinction worth having. Obviously the goods of life brought into being in this effort for distinction are on the credit side of life. But where the finer ability for serviceable distinction is lacking, another principle of distinction has developed, that of ability to waste. As Veblen pointed out in his *Theory of the Leisure Class*, one frequent sign of social superiority is the ability to possess and consume beyond organic needs.

It would be a mistake, however, to believe that this principle of conspicuous waste exhibits itself only in the life of socially superior persons. By the law of imitation, it runs through all orders of society, so that the poor man in his lesser way buys for display rather than for service.

Summing up, then, we note that just as on the side of production not all effort is cost, so on the side of consumption not all consumption goods count as utility.

FORMULATING A HUMAN INTERPRETATION

The fundamental economic principle is that of maximizing utility and minimizing cost. We are now able, in terms of the foregoing analysis, Hobson believed, to formulate a more broadly human interpretation of this principle. It is obvious that from the standpoint of traditional economic science, the maximization of utility can mean only increased production of consumables, while the minimization of cost can mean only the diminution of effort expended in their production. More goods and less work. From the standpoint of a humanized economics, however, maximization of utility means on the one hand such an organization of industrial processes that all the work done enlists as far as possible the intrinsic power and interest of each worker; it means on the other hand such production and distribution of consumption-goods as meet most thoroughly the organic needs of those who consume. Minimization of cost signifies the elimination as far as possible of such kinds of work as hinder the development of the intrinsic power and interest of each worker; it signifies also the elimination of such consumption-goods and of such methods of distribution as go counter to true organic needs. In other words, a thoroughly humanized society, he felt, will see to it that each member is enabled first to contribute in accordance with his fundamental ability to do so, and secondly, to receive in accordance with his fundamental needs.

This interpretation at once clarifies the whole distribution problem. Shall men receive in proportion to what they produce? Then we fail wholly to take account of the two facts: (1) that what is produced may, socially speaking, not be worth producing; and (2) that the production may be carried on in ways injurious to human welfare. Or shall men receive in proportion to the efforts they expend? Again, the fact is patent that efforts, however laborious or painful, may be misdirected, while well-directed efforts may be full of stimulus and joy. The only organic principle of distribution, in short, is that which is based wholly on fundamental needs. Such a principle not only provides against mal-distribution—the assigning of less than the needs of individual demands—but provides likewise against mal-production—the creation of goods that go counter to organic needs. When, moreover, it is recognized, as properly it must be, that a man's needs include work of a nature to draw out his unique powers, the "needs" principle of distribution calls for the complete development in all persons of their essential powers.

CONCLUSION

It is apparent how, through such a humanizing of the traditional economic definitions of utility, cost, and value as Hobson suggested, a far clearer grasp is made possible of the principles which should in a future society govern production, consumption, and distribution. When and as economics advances to such a broadening and deepening of its concepts, it may properly begin to direct the organization of our material life. But until it does so advance beyond its traditional pecuniary abstractions, its judgments will possess the lack of wisdom which attaches to every point of view that fails to take into account all the factors essential to the human situation.

CHAPTER 10. WHEN JUSTICE BECOMES INJUSTICE

THE chief and captain of the difficulties in our legal system lies in a certain philosophy which for two centuries at least has played an important part in our common law and which has been adopted by Americans as peculiarly expressive of their social and political thought. This may indeed seem strange, that a philosophy should be the cause of legal ills; for to most of us, doubtless, philosophies are of the insubstantial stuff of dreams and have little bearing upon practical life. But the fact remains that not only has this certain philosophy determined many of our judicial decisions, but it has done so in a manner so widely disastrous that it has long roused indignant protest among us.

The English common law, in which this philosophy has prominent part, for many centuries served the high purpose of defending liberty against despotic oppression. Its principle of "the supremacy of the law" was construed for the sake of guarding individual rights against the arbitrary will of other individuals or powers. It had its strong development in centuries when, by reason of the aristocratic and theocratic organization of society, the oppression of the individual was relatively easy—the oppression of him bodily, or through his property, or family affections, or religious convictions. In such an age, the defense of the individual had to be secured by law expressing unequivocally and emphatically the sacredness of certain individual rights. Thomas More gave expression to this in the then revolutionary principle that in an ideal state all individuals must be equal before the law.

But it was increasingly realized by the social philosophers of those centuries that opposition to the two strongly intrenched classes—the clergy and the nobility—to be successful, must be founded upon wholly unassailable principles. Those rights of the common man which the law was seeking to defend must be shown to be grounded not in anything so capricious and open to doubt as the will of legislators, but in the very nature of reality itself. For the privileged classes might easily retort that it was not socially expedient to regard all men as equal before the law. Aristotle, for example, had reasoned that certain persons were naturally slaves. A society organized according to a graduated system of special hereditary privileges would, according to him, offer far more promise of a brilliant development than one in which the highest in birth and accomplishment was regarded legally as having no more rights than the lowest. Thus, to the social philosophers intent upon undermining the system of class privilege there was apparently but one course to pursue: to prove that the equality of all men, their possession of certain unassailable rights irrespective of class or station, was grounded in nature itself. So to the end of defending the common man and of abrogating special privileges and immunities, the philosophical theory of natural rights was slowly wrought into shape. This is the theory which is still the basis of our American legal and constitutional systems.

It will be unnecessary here to enter into a detailed history of the development of this social theory. It will suffice to recall its main points: (1) that all men are born free and politically equal, and that it is their natural right therefore to remain thus free and equal; (2) that since men are by natural right equal, no one can have any right to encroach on another's equal right, among these rights being those of life, liberty, property, and the pursuit of happiness; (3) that political rights are based upon contract.

The first two principles are sufficiently familiar. The third, which is their logical outcome and which has brought in its train most of the difficulties since encountered, is not so familiar. According to the theory of equal birth and equal right, the individual is the primordial unit. All institutions, organizations, societies are secondary to him, have their growth out of him. The state therefore is but the product of individual wills; the individual is in no sense the product of the state. The state exists to serve these primordial wills; it must in no wise encroach upon them save as they have themselves, for their own advantage, consented to such encroachment. Whatever powers therefore the state possesses are powers granted to it by individuals. The state, in short, is wholly the result of the mutual consent or contract of the individuals to enter into community of life. From this point of view the state is, as it were, a necessary evil. It is simply the surrendered residuum of individual rights and privileges.

It follows from this view that the power and authority

of the state are to be jealously restricted. The prime concern of men is the preservation of the rights and privileges of each individual. We find a vivid expression of this individualism in a typical passage from Blackstone: "So great moreover is the regard of law for private property, that it will not authorize the least violation of it; no not even for the general good of the whole community. If a new road, for instance, were to be made through the grounds of a private person, it might perhaps be extensively beneficial to the public, but the law permits no man, or set of men, to do this without the consent of the owner of the land. In vain it may be urged that the good of the individual ought to yield to that of the community, for it would be dangerous to allow any private man, or even any public tribunal, to be the judge of this common good, or to decide whether it is expedient or no. Besides, the public good is in nothing more essentially interested than in the protection of every individual's private right." [1]

In the light of historical conditions, it is not difficult to explain such a view, so jealously careful of individual rights, so suspicious of governmental encroachment. The explanation will be found to have important bearing upon our own peculiar attitude toward governmental interference with the rights of individuals. "The eighteenth century conception of liberty," writes Professor J. Allen Smith,[2] "was the outgrowth of the political conditions of that time. Government was largely in the hands of a rul-

[1] Blackstone, *Commentaries* (Wendell), page 138.

[2] *The Spirit of American Government*, page 291 (The Macmillan Company).

ing class who were able to further their own interest at the expense of the many who were unrepresented. It was but natural under these circumstances that the people should seek to limit the exercise of political authority, since every check imposed upon the government lessened the dangers of class rule." There was every reason, then, why the common man should be suspicious of government, and why the English common law, developed in large measure to protect him, should lay stress upon his individual right against the relatively irresponsible power of the ruling classes.

It was in this thought of individual freedom from governmental control that our American nation was born. There was the memory of aristocratic oppression, political and clerical, and the thought of government as the ready instrument of such oppression. To secure liberty, then, meant to secure the individual against political domination. Government was indeed a necessity even for freedom; but the less one had of it the better. This accounts largely for the extreme care with which the founders of our nation guarded themselves against political encroachment, hedged the state about with all manner of restrictions, and surrounded their individual rights and liberties with secure protective devices. Government was to be feared—for had it not always been the source and instrument of privileged oppression?

Yet, curiously enough, in the brief period of our national existence, the situation has become almost exactly reversed. In the eighteenth century the political order was oligarchic, while the economic order was democratic—small producers and manufacturers, an easy transition from employee to employer, wealth very widely distributed, economic opportunities relatively equal. The hope of the members of that democratic economic order was to be let alone by the oligarchic governmental order. *Laissez faire* was the solvent word. In the nineteenth and twentieth centuries, on the contrary, the conditions have been very nearly exactly reversed. The economic order is now the conspicuously oligarchic order: through the introduction of complex machinery and the concentration of industries, the small producers and manufacturers have been swept largely into the class of hired workers; a wide gulf yawns between employers and employees; the employee may no longer easily become an employer; wealth is concentrated in the hands of a few; economic opportunities are exceedingly unequal. The industrial revolution, in short, "has resulted in the transfer of industrial power from the many to the few, who now exercise in all matters relating to production an authority as absolute and irresponsible as that which the ruling classes exercised in the middle of the eighteenth century over the state itself." [3] As against this development of oligarchic organization in the economic order, there is, on the contrary, in the political order increasing realization of democratic equality. Thus the social group which is now a danger to the liberty of the common man is no longer, as in the former centuries, the political ruling class, for in our political democracy we have no class with special political privileges. It is the economically regnant class. I need not dwell upon this. There will be no question, I think, that the chief threat to our demo-

[3] *Ibid.*, page 307.

cratic institutions today is the vast economic powers which tend more and more to override our legislatures, to defy our common will, to suppress the sovereign rule of the people by the more powerful sovereignty of economic compulsion. More and more the political state, once supreme, tends to become but a lesser state within a state.

MISAPPLIED JUSTICE

And now we may perhaps realize the curious contradiction in which, as a nation, we have found ourselves. The theory of natural rights, fashioned in the years when the state was the natural foe and the economic order was the refuge of the common man, is still our national theory in the day when, on the contrary, the state is the refuge and the economic order is in many respects the chief foe of the common man. In the earlier century the cry of "hands off business" was the slogan of individual liberty; in the later nineteenth and the twentieth centuries it is the slogan of economic organizations that control individual liberty. It is not surprising then that a theory embodied in the common law and stated expressly in the Constitution, which once served for the protection of the common man, has become increasingly the instrument of his oppression. As a distinguished jurist has expressed it, "Today for the first time the common law finds itself arrayed against the people; for the first time, instead of securing for them what they most prize, they know it chiefly as something that continually stands between them and what they desire. . . . There is a feeling that [the common law] prevents everything and does nothing. . . . It exhibits too great a respect for the individual and for the intrenched position in which our legal and political history has put him, and too little respect for the needs of society, when they come in conflict with the individual, to be in touch with the present age."[4]

This reversal of the situation may be aptly illustrated by reference to decisions of our high courts of appeal. To take a famous instance, a law was passed prohibiting the manufacturing of cigars in the home. It was obviously a law framed in view, not only of social welfare, but of the welfare of those whom it prohibited from sweatshop work. Yet a high court of appeal pronounced the law unconstitutional. Its reason for so doing was that such a law restricted the workman in his liberty of choice as to the place and manner in which he was to earn a livelihood. "Liberty in its broad sense as understood in this country," said Justice Earl in his decision in this case, "means the right not only of freedom from actual servitude, imprisonment, or restraint, but the right of one to use his faculties in all lawful ways, to live and work where he will, to earn his livelihood in any lawful calling, and to pursue any lawful trade or avocation. All laws, therefore, which impair or trammel these rights (except as such laws may be passed in the exercise by the legislature of the police powers . . .), are infringements upon his fundamental rights of liberty, which are under constitutional protection."

It is true, indeed, that by such a decision of the court, the

[4] Pound, R., *Do We Need a Philosophy of Law?* Col. Law Rev., Vol. V, page 344. May, 1905.

individual's liberty was protected against the encroachment of the state. But in this case the real enemy was not the state, but exploiting manufacturers. Thus the court, in protecting the worker against his apparent enemy, actually delivered him bound hand and foot to his real foe, the sweatshop manufacturer, and this in the sacred name of protection to the worker's fundamental rights.

Again an act was passed by a legislative body prohibiting the payment of workmen in anything except money. Speaking of these sections of the act, the court said:[5] "They are wholly unconstitutional and void, inasmuch as by them an attempt has been made by the legislature to do what in this country can not be done; that is, prevent persons who are *sui juris* from making their own contracts. The act is an infringement alike of the right of the employer and the employee. He may sell his labor for what he thinks best, whether money or goods, just as his employer may sell his iron and coal, and any and every law that proposes to prevent him from so doing is an infringement of his constitutional privileges and is consequently vicious and void."

Here again the court was ostensibly defending the right of the individual laborer, placing him as a free individual with "rights" on a par with his employer. But who that has known the viciousness of the widespread system of payment in company orders or in truck store goods or in forms of vague promises, and who that has known the weakness of the individual laborer to protest against such payment, does not realize that such ostensible court protection ex-

[5] Godcharles and Wigeman, 113 Pa. St., 431.

posed the worker but the more fatally to the oppression of unscrupulous employers?

Again an act was passed restricting the number of hours of work per day to eight. (*Ex parte* Kubach, 85 Col. 274.) The court pronounced this null and void, supporting its decision as follows: "We can not conceive of any theory upon which a city could be justified in making it a misdemeanor for one of its citizens to contract with another for services to be rendered because the contract is that he shall work for more than a limited number of hours." Again the decision was in a wholly individualistic spirit. There was no thought that the permission given to each individual to contract as he pleased as to number of hours was really a power given to employing agencies to compel as long hours of labor as they possibly could. Again in this case it was the legislature that sought to protect the common man, while it was the court that, protesting against legislative interference with his individual "rights," in fact exposed the man to the exploitation of employers. The court, curiously enough, thus made it necessary for the worker, if he would defend himself against exploitation, to do so by extra-legal methods of trade-union pressure. And yet when such pressure was brought to bear, the courts were swift to issue summary injunctions.

Again an act was passed requiring that wages due be paid on the day of discharge. The court pronounced this act null and void; and in so doing declared with eloquent indignation: [6] "The patrimony of the poor man lies in the strength and dexterity of his own hands; and to hinder

[6] Leep v. St. Louis I.M. & S.R. Co. (1894); 58 Ark. 407.

him from employing these in what manner he may think proper, without injury to his neighbors, is a plain violation of this most sacred property." Therefore, said the court in effect, the poor man must never be deprived of the inestimable privilege of agreeing with his employer to wait patiently six months or even a year or a dozen years for the money justly due him at the time of his discharge. *Summa jus summa injuria!*

One might easily multiply instances, but the foregoing are typical of many decisions.

In all these cases the object of the court was perfectly clear and the procedure perfectly legal: to protect the individual in his right freely to contract, to prevent any encroachment upon this fundamental right of his on the part of the state. This protection was granted on the theory that the individual had a natural right to the ownership and disposal of his private property—his property in things or in his labor. But wholly absent from these decisions, as we have seen, was the thought that the real encroacher was not the state, but the economic power against which the state directs its legislation. "I do not criticize these decisions," writes Dean Pound, after detailing a score or more of them. "As the law stands, I do not doubt they were rightly determined. But they serve to show that the right of the individual to contract as he pleases is upheld by our legal system at the expense of the right of society to stand between our laboring population and oppression. This right of the individual and this exaggerated respect for his right are common-law doctrines. And this means that a struggle is in progress between society and the common law."

LIVING WITH A SELF-CONTRADICTION

It is in this conception of the individual's natural right to the unrestricted ownership, use, and disposal of his property, and to his freedom therein from state interference, that the crux of our American difficulty has lain. It is in this conception, too, that the theory of "natural rights" has come into direct conflict with its own more essential principles. For among the other "natural rights," the theory assumes men to possess the rights of life, liberty, and the pursuit of happiness. We have just seen how the strict carrying out of the principle of the inviolability of private property (that is, in the right freely to contract) came into conflict with the industrial liberty of workers, with their pursuit of happiness, and, too often, with their life itself. In the earlier centuries, as we have seen, such a conflict could hardly occur by reason of the relative equality of men in the economic order.

Our present American situation, therefore, owing to important changes in economic conditions, has shown forth as never before the fundamental self-contradition hitherto lurking in the theory of natural rights. The difficulty of the situation has lain in the fact that, because the American Constitution which embodies this self-contradictory theory has been practically unchangeable, and because the courts are sworn to the service of that Constitution, our American life has had to subject itself to the curious indignity of ruling itself by laws and principles patently self-contradictory.

THE NEED FOR A NEW SOCIAL PHILOSOPHY

What then of the remedy? Obviously, it must lie in such modification of the philosophy which has been at the foundation of our legal system as will eliminate the patent self-contradictions. How is such modification to be accomplished? Let us regard in this connection two remedies that have been, at times, proposed as a cure for our legal and political difficulties: the recall of judges and the recall of decisions. Would these remedies really cure the evils? That they would cure some evils, one may easily believe, although one may easily be certain, too, that one of them at least would bring distempers greater than the evils cured.

Would the recall of judges solve our difficulties? It might indeed be effective in eliminating certain forms of personal corruption; but it could hardly be effective in overcoming the legal self-contradiction of which we have spoken. For the judges who would replace those dismissed would be men trained in the same legal theories, and inevitably responsive to the same legal philosophy. Besides, they would be in sworn service to a constitution which expressly embodies that philosophy.

Would the recall of judicial decisions effect a cure? Here we come, I think, to the root of the question. However great the evils which such recall would bring in its train, it might indeed be effective if we as a nation were ourselves conscious of a solvent social philosophy. But we are not. We are vaguely, more or less distressfully, aware that something is amiss; that we have not, often, the legislative right to accomplish what we desire to accomplish; that liberty goes hand in hand with servitude, and the rights of man with oppression. But what is the fundamental reason for it, and what is the way out, the American people for the most part simply do not know. Thus granting that we had recalled the decisions—decisions rendered in faithful accord with our accepted national philosophy—we should ourselves have no coherent legal, political, or economic philosophy to offer in terms of which later decisions might be more adequately rendered. The fact is, in short, that our normal American life exhibits the very self-contradictions found in our national philosophy. We believe implicitly—most of us—in the inviolable rights of private property even at the very moment when we realize the havoc to social welfare wrought by that theory of inviolability.

To whom, for example, belong the inviolable rights of property—to the owner of various forms of capital, or to the owner of labor? If inviolability means unrestricted possession and use, then both of these rights cannot be equally inviolable; for one of them, as we know—labor—is easily forced into submission by the other. What is, then, the true relation between the inviolability of a man's property in his labor and the inviolability of a man's property in his capital? The two inviolabilities would seem to be inherently in conflict.

Is the equitable relation between them that of a drawn

battle—the property in capital, on the one side, and the property in labor on the other? Shall the state, then, recognizing the drawn battle, recognize the right of the laborer to organize for such battle? And if it recognizes this right of industrial organization, shall it protect him against persecution by employers for exercising this right in times of industrial peace? Or shall the state frown upon such extra-legal methods of adjustment and either leave the individual owner of labor to his individual fate, or secure his labor rights, as to hours and wage, through legislation? As to all this we are in doubt. Our court decisions are now one way and now another.

Or is the difficulty still deeper? Does the inviolable right to one kind of ownership—that of capital—grant to such ownership a wholly disproportionate power—first, to extort more than its fair share of reward, and, secondly, to influence legislative bodies to the end of preventing the passage of laws curtailing that power? And is the way out of this difficulty, the removal, as far as possible, of such ownership from private to public hands?

In this matter, we as a people are still almost wholly at sea. And our courts drift as we drift, now to this compromise, now to that.

THE NEW NEED

Our deepest task, today, in short, is the achievement of an economic and legal philosophy that will be adequate to the full demands of a democratic civilization. To a degree, we have wrought out a philosophy of political democracy. For a while we accounted that sufficient. But we have been realizing increasingly through the sad and somewhat terrifying lessons of legislatures debauched by private enterprises, of courts owned and controlled, of political parties the subservient tools of the regnant economic powers, that political democracy is in fact impossible of achievement where there is not present a like democracy in the economic life of a people. But what are we to mean by economic or industrial democracy? Apparently we, as a people, simply do not know. Thus there continues in our national life this conflict between undemocratic beliefs and behaviors in our economic life, on the one hand, and our fundamental democratic ideals, on the other; and it is this conflict that leaves us distressed and unwitting of our way.

More fundamental therefore than any of the reforms in our political or legal machinery is the reform in our national social philosophy, particularly in that aspect of it which is concerned with the idea of property. How to democratize and socialize ownership? And yet, with all our present vagueness, there can be no question, I think, that such a reform of our national philosophy is in process. Reforms of this kind are not made by single men, though often the single man creates the trenchant formulation, nor are they created by legislative pronouncements. They occur as a result of increasing pressure of widespread social difficulties and through the gradual awakening of men to new social needs. Such is the condition in our present day. The well-nigh universal, ofttimes violent criticism of our courts, where our undemocratic economic philosophy is displayed in its most uncompromising form, the weepings and gnashings of teeth over decisions that hinder the prosecution of our earnest endeavors for human welfare, are indications of our growing dissatisfaction with the national theory that is ours. We launch out indeed against the courts, but all the while we are, in fact, launching out against the inadequacies of our national philosophy. Gradually we are framing for ourselves a new theory of law, economics, and politics. It is for this reason, above all, that public criticism of the courts as well as of our constitutional government, instead of being hushed as unseemly, should be welcomed as the surest, healthiest means of the nation's emancipation from old doctrines and of its education to a more adequate economic, political, and legal point of view.

Again the great unrest in the economic world, the growing recognition of the necessity for curbing economic domination, of controlling, indeed of abrogating certain types of ownership, is clarifying the national consciousness both as to the character of this more fundamental problem and the way of its solution.

AN EMERGING PHILOSOPHY

There can be no question that a new social philosphy of great import for democratic civilization is to be the outcome of this period of stress and storm. To this new social synthesis the vast and for the most part still ill-assorted results of modern economists, sociologists, social psychologists, political scientists, moralists, and philosophical jurists will be the essential contribution. It is not altogether improbable that we shall live to see the day when out of the conflicts and contradictions, the confusions and misunderstandings of the present there will rise a nationally accepted philosophy of social and economic—not simply of political—democracy, momentous to the coming centuries as was the philosophy of Rousseau to popular sovereignty, of Grotius to international law, of Locke to civil and religious liberty. There is here a fascinating task for the philosopher of the present and the future—to grasp the essential contradictions of our present social order, and out of their members to help rear the structure of a more adequate social theory.

Our chief task today, in short, should be an examination into the nature of our fundamental social thought—political, legal, and economic. Before it, all the temporary tinkerings with this bit of machinery and that sink into insignificance. The day is ripe for a new, deepened conception of human rights and obligations, for a solvent thought that will remove what is no longer trustworthy in the old conceptions of liberty and property, labor and wage, and in their place rear a firmer, more truly grounded structure of democratic mutuality. It is significant to note the confirmation of this view by a group of our leading teachers of law. In the General Introduction of the *Modern Legal Philosophy Series*, issued by a committee of the Association of American Law Schools, we find the following: " 'Until either philosophers become kings,' said Socrates, 'or kings philosophers, states will never succeed in remedying their shortcomings.' And if he was loath to give forth this view, because, as he admitted, it might 'sink him beneath the waters of laughter and ridicule,' so today among us it would doubtless resound in folly if we sought to apply it again in our own fields of state life, and to assert that philosophers must become lawyers or lawyers philosophers, if our law is ever to be advanced into its perfect working.

"And yet there is hope, as there is need, among us today, of some such transformation. Of course history shows that there have always been cycles of legal progress, and that they have often been heralded and guided by philosophies. But particularly there is hope that our own people may be the generation now about to exemplify this."

CHAPTER 11. THE GOVERNMENT OF TOMORROW

THE problem of political reconstruction is a vital one in our American life. Only recently, we have witnessed the relief which a whole people has felt at an unprecedented concentration of power in a single individual. The relief has expressed the extent of our lack of confidence in the constituted legislative bodies. Why was there this lack of confidence? The case was not an isolated one. For years our distrust of political bodies has been growing, until it has become a commonplace among us not to expect either wisdom or efficiency in our political governors. Coupled with this distrust is the bewildering feeling that we cannot do anything about it. Even though we conscientiously go to the polls, we invariably find ourselves unable to alter the typical situation. Whether in city or state or nation, we put in our votes and pull out the same disappointing aggregations of mediocrity and inefficiency.

Why is this so? An analysis of our political situation would seem to lead to the conviction that political bodies are inefficient because there is something amiss in the political mechanism we are employing. It is as if a man were compelled to paint a portrait with a toothbrush, or trim a garden lawn with a pocket-knife. In brief, we are operating with a system that in many respects is inadequate to the task set before it. The first step toward political reconstruction, therefore, is to examine this curiously inept mechanism and see whether it cannot be made more nearly to comply with modern conditions and demands of life.

ARTIFICIAL GROUPING

One of the most serious defects of our political machinery appears in the prevalent theory of representation. It is curious how we accept that theory as if it had been handed to us from Sinai's top, not noting that the times have so changed as to make it no longer successfully applicable. We view it as a matter of course that a political state should be divided into its smaller units, these into still smaller units, and these, in turn, into still smaller; and that in each, citizens should vote as members of the unit. Thus the group of people who constitute a certain precinct of a certain district of the borough of Manhattan recognize, as a matter of course, that their political identity lies in their membership within those territorial boundaries. The person who "represents" these citizens represents them as inhabitants of this particular territory.

Amid all the serious questioning of our political procedures, it is curious that this system of territorial division and territorial representation is accepted practically without question. And yet it is not an exaggeration to say that of all features of our political life, it is the one that is most distinctly out of date and the source of the most serious political drawbacks. It is not difficult to realize that at one time in the history of society such a system was the only one that could work with secure and comprehensive success. In a community thoroughly agricultural, for example, similarity of interest was in the main identical with spacial propinquity. If, in such a community, one were to district off a square mile of inhabitants, one would find that within that square mile the interests were fundamentally alike. If one were to take another square mile a hundred or a thousand miles away, one would find, indeed, that the interests differed somewhat from those within the first square mile—the difference between wheat-land interests, for example, and grazing-land interests—but within the second square mile one would again find the interests substantially alike.

These facts gave the territorial plan of political districting its erstwhile excuse for being. But suppose that in a manufacturing and commercial community of today, one districts off a square mile of inhabitants. Within the boundaries of that domain one finds a barber living next to a grocer, a grocer next to a real-estate broker, a real-estate broker next to a school teacher, a school teacher next to a keeper of a speakeasy, a keeper of a speakeasy next to a mason, a mason next to an actor, and so forth. Within the square mile, in brief, are interests as far apart as they possibly can be; and yet our political system operates upon the supposition that this heterogeneous mass of beings can be swept into unity by the mere fiction of a political demarcation. On election day, these heterogeneous folk are asked to come together and vote for some person to represent their "common" interests. Obviously, they have no "common" interests, save the sheerest matters of external life. They can have no common enthusiasm, no common will for something socially fine and inspiring. Their "common" will, in short, is nothing but the common denominator of all their diverse interests—a denominator that is the lower the more diverse the interests; and this lowest common denominator becomes incarnate in the politician.

Social interest and effectiveness can be evoked only where there is a spirit of the group. But a spirit of the group can be generated only where men feel that they have similar interests. Men thrown accidentally together by the chance renting of this apartment or that house cannot be made to feel that they have interests in common if both their vocations and avocations carry them in widely different directions. Herein lies the typical defect of our modern political system. It attempts, in short, to bring into expression group-loyalties and group-judgments when the groups through which it operates are inevitably artificial. Apparently there is no cure for this, save as we face the issue of organizing political life into its common-interest groups.

TOWARD COMMON-INTEREST GROUPING

What are these common-interest groups? The answer to this question has been different in different periods of history. In the earliest period the common-interest groups were those of kinship. Men felt that they belonged together because they were born of some common ancestor. All the aspects of their life—political, economic, religious

—were organized in terms of the blood bond. It is not difficult to understand why this was so. The first period of human history was that of hunting. Men wandered about from place to place in search of game. Obviously, the only bond was that of procreation. So strong was this that neither distance nor fortune could weaken its hold. The members of a tribe might be scattered to the four winds of heaven; they were nevertheless members of the tribe.

The second stage of human history introduced a factor which was destined, ere long, to supersede the kinship bond as the principle of grouping—that of territorial occupation. When men learned how to plant and reap, a new chapter of political history was opened. Gradually—though only at first under stress of conflict with the kinship-principle—the principle of territorial grouping took its place as the great formative factor in social and political life. The history of modern society is that of the slow supersession of the kinship by the territorial bond.

In the modern citizen-state the kinship bond has been completely superseded. Men now belong to a political group not by reason of their descent but by reason of their settled location in a certain territory.

Is the evolution complete, or may we look to a further development of political grouping? The groupings of the past were determined by the nature of men's occupations. For the huntsman, life was a roving; and the only possible bond of union was the impalpable bond of descent. For the agriculturist, life was a settled occupancy in which the bond of union was the palpable one of land. Are men in large measure changing the nature of their occupations?

The answer is clear. Agriculture, while still fundamental, is increasingly supplemented by occupations that make profound alterations in our life. Indeed, the present age is one not of agricultural but of manufacturing and commercial economy. If, then, the change from hunting to agriculture brought about a transformation of the principle of political grouping, may we not expect that the change from the agricultural to the manufacturing and commercial economy will effect a transformation of equal moment?

At the present time territorial propinquity is no longer coincident with community of occupational interest. This change is crucial. It means that where political life could once be successfully organized in terms of land occupation, such organization is now in large measure artificial and ineffective. Community of interest is now, as ever, determined fundamentally by vocation. A physician living in the eleventh precinct has far more community of interest with a physician living in the fifth precinct than he has with the theatrical manager who lives around the corner. If one were to trace the lines of occupational-interest demarcation in a city, one would find them here, there, and everywhere, crossing and recrossing all the conventional political boundaries. If one seeks, in short, the common-interest groupings in our modern world, one finds them in the associations of teachers, of merchants, of manufacturers, of physicians, of artisans. The Trades Union, the Chamber of Commerce, the Medical Association, the Bar Association, the Housewives' League—these apparently are the forerunners of the political units of the modern state.

A FALSE PSYCHOLOGICAL CONDITION

Always, in history, political effectiveness has had its source in common understanding and common interest. Where men work at the same trade or pursue the same business or follow the same profession, there is an identity of interest that makes for a certain group solidarity and power. A perfectly clear principle of psychology is here involved. Where two or three are gathered together who are of widely diverse interests, there can be little save trivial talk of the times and of the weather. When, on the contrary, there are gathered together those who are of similar interest and understanding, there results a mutual enhancement which makes for the greater power of each and of all. The weakness and timid superficiality of our political life today are due, in large measure, to the fact that the political state is made up of groups of the first—the talk-of-the-weather type. Our political life will apparently come to genuine power only when the state is transformed into groups of the second—the common-interest—type.

Anyone who has had the least experience in practical politics knows how disheartening to a citizen earnest for political welfare is an ordinary election. There is the strenuous attempt to persuade every Tom, Dick, and Harry to come into one's appointed camp. It is not that the Toms, Dicks, and Harrys are not worthy persons, nor that one is contaminating oneself in associating with them. It is rather that the whole process is psychologically hopeless and socially wasteful. One realizes always that these heterogeneous citizens really have no awareness of anything in common. One realizes that even with the prerogative of the vote in their hands, their wishes are foisted upon them and must continue to be foisted as long as the political system compels such ill-assorted citizens to dwell politically together. One notes, with some cynicism, that exercise of the suffrage, under the present artificial conditions, is regarded by the good citizen as a largely ineffective obligation that must nevertheless be performed; and by the bad citizen as one that can be turned to lucrative purposes. Seldom does the campaigner witness within one area a solid group that is aware of itself and of its ideals, that can be counted upon to work year after year for that which it holds good. The only solid groups he finds are those which work profitably for that which is accounted socially and politically evil.

EFFECT OF COMMON-INTEREST GROUPING

The ways of life have changed fundamentally, and political organization must, if it is to be effective, accommodate itself to the change. Sir Henry Maine, after reciting the fact that the "history of political ideas begins . . . with the assumption that kinship in blood is the sole possible ground of community in political functions," goes on to say, "nor are there any of those subversions of feeling, which we term emphatically revolutions, so startling and so complete as the change which is accomplished when some other principle—such as that, for example, of local contiguity—establishes itself for the first time as the basis of political action." One always invites suspicion when one declares or prophesies a revolution. Yet with Sir Henry Maine in support of the assumption, one may confidently declare that the second great political revolution is even now in prospect—the change from the territorial to the functional basis of political grouping.

That this change, perplexing as will be the problems it will generate, will mean much for our political life cannot, I think, be doubted. Of primary importance will be the fact that the basis of selection of candidates will be both logically and psychologically superior to that of the present system. A group of a hundred physicians or of a hundred teachers or of a hundred artisans would be far more capable of making secure judgment upon one of its number than a helter-skelter group of citizens selected according to locality. Again, for a man desirous of serving the public welfare, there would be a peculiar pleasure in standing for the fellows of his craft or profession. His appeal to them for support would be an appeal to their understanding and to their intelligent interests. There would be no need for him to lower himself to that type of campaign cajolery which is necessary, apparently, when the appeal must be made to all sorts and conditions of men. It is precisely the undignified character of the prevalent political methods of campaigning that deters many an interested person from offering service to the public—the printing of one's photograph on cards, the widespread distribution of self-laudatory handbills, the posting of conspicuous placards, the ringing of innumerable door-bells, the whole sorry business, in short, of making oneself a general public nuisance, of doing what any decently self-respecting man would in ordinary circumstances shrink from doing. But to offer oneself to the fellows of one's craft or profession—that is a far different matter. One comes then not as a stranger. One comes as a worker, known among fellow workers. One has not to force onself, as it were, down the throats of the indifferent and the unknowing. One stands on one's reputation; and one is accepted or rejected as that reputation is taken to be honorable or not. The whole spirit of elections, in short, would tend to change from an undignified attempt to wheedle and cajole men into a transient support, into a self-respecting expression of willingness to serve one's fellowmen.

But another important change would be in evidence. If one asks what the vital interests are that deserve representation in government, one may not stop short of enumerating all the occupations fundamental to our modern life. Education is fundamental, medicine, law, housewifery, commerce, manufacturing, carpentering, bricklaying, and so forth. How many of these get effective expression in our present type of government? Where is the voice of the physician speaking for that fraternity whose interest is in public health, in hygiene, sanitation, wholesome working conditions, protection of children? Where is the voice of the teacher speaking for that group whose interest is in the mental and moral equipment of children? Where is the voice of the housewife speaking for the great body of women whose interest is in the health and decency of the home, in the nurture of children, in the heightening and enriching of life? Where is the voice of the artist speaking for those who love the beautiful? Government, as it is organized today, has no place for these save by indirection. If education, or medicine, or housewifery or art would be heard in the halls of legislation, they must say their words into the half-understanding ears of some ambitious lawyer who will later reproduce them in his own way—if the times and the occasions fit.

Here is the baffling aspect of our modern political life, that with all the diverse interests that need expression, all expression is barred save, in the main, as it issues from the lips of a lawyer or a business man. There can be no proper political life—none, that is, adequate to the rich variety of our social existence—until this rulership of the lawyer and the business man is abolished, until all authentic interests, in short, speak their needful words in their own proper character.

The politician, for the most part, is the logical outcome of the out-of-date system in which we find ourselves. He is the man who can move easily among a heterogeneous citizenry, glib of tongue, genial of hand, easy at all problems, master of none. The incarnation of that conceptual monstrosity, "the average citizen," he fills our legislative halls with eloquence and incompetence. There is apparently no hope for our politics until we are able to rid ourselves of him. Obviously we shall accomplish the removal only as we alter the basis of our political selection, so that it enables us to choose not a hail-fellow from among a heterogeneous mass but a representative from a functional group.

One other possible advantage is to be noted. Grouping by occupation would in large measure solve the vexed problem of sex discrimination in political participation. Adult persons—irrespective of sex—will have their political identity in terms of the functional interests they serve. It is untrue, for example, to suppose that a Tammany lawyer knows as much about the interests of the housewife group as the housewives themselves. Housewifery is an interest fundamental to civilized society. It should therefore have its competent representatives in the chambers of social legislation. But note that in the new type of grouping the housewife will assume her political functions not as one who is competent to judge upon all matters of public import, but as one who brings to political life her peculiar and expert contribution.

TOWARD FUNCTIONAL GOVERNMENT

A prophet may maintain himself in esteem as long as he confines his prophecies to generalities. When, on the contrary, he essays particulars, his prophet's garb too often turns into the motley of the fool. The writer will most effectively escape unnecessary embarrassment, then, if he refrains from detailed elaboration. And yet, for the sake of clearness, a word or two must be said with regard to particulars of organization. Two problems come prominently to the front in any such grouping as that suggested: first, the problem concerning the lines of group demarcation; second, the problem arising out of a conflict of interests.

As to the first problem, it seems clear that all sharply marked occupational differences must be accepted as lines of political grouping. Thus teachers are sharply marked as over against physicians, housewives as over against outdoor unskilled laborers. In any community, one would be able to divide the adult inhabitants into groups very much as follows: teachers, merchants, manufacturers, engineers, artists (including architects, novelists, poets, musicians), newspaper writers, indoor unskilled manual workers, outdoor unskilled manual workers, housewives, physicians, farmers, lawyers, ministers, public guards (police, firemen, soldiers). This cannot pretend to be an accurate or final analysis of the grouping possibilities of a community, but along some such lines the grouping would proceed.

As to the second problem, the objection is often raised that occupational grouping would simply mean a battle of interests—each group fighting for itself. But in this respect matters could scarcely be worse than they now are. Moreover, groups such as we have indicated, are not always antagonistic in their interests. Housewives are not necessarily antagonistic to physicians; nor carpenters to teachers; nor ministers of religion to outdoor unskilled workers. As a matter of fact, the interests of many of these groups frequently coalesce, as in the case of housewives, teachers, physicians. But, with as many occupational groups as we have indicated, no constant balancing of interests one against the other would be possible, and while it is true that the ancient process of log-rolling would not be absent, for it is doubtless part of the nature of man as a "political animal," it would be carried on under conditions where there would be a far more effective check in favor of valid social interest than where two parties with no essential difference of point of view strive for control of the spoils.

THE ORGANIC STATE

The foregoing pages express a view of political participation which is in keeping with the organic nature of the state. In an organism, each part or member contributes in accordance with its powers—the heart cells as members of the heart group, the epithelial cells as members of the epithelial group. The nerve cells run here and there throughout the body; yet they contribute not in terms of their locality—whether they happen to live in the hands or heart—but in terms of their functional activity, their "organic occupation." The present form of suffrage grouping, on the other hand, is distictly anorganic. The state is conceived as very much like a heap of sand, each grain like every other grain, each contributing in like manner and measure to the aggregate whole. But nothing is clearer than the fact that not all persons can contribute in equal measure or with like quality of interest and expertness to the state. Where some are utterly ignorant of matters vital to the state, others, through their daily occupations, are equipped with expert knowledge. It is because our modern democracy treats all individuals as abstractly alike, because, in short, it does not regard them as persons with functional differences, that it fails so conspicuously to elicit from its members their best abilities and efforts.

It would be folly to pretend that a high grade of political efficiency will be attained at once if and when men change from the non-organic system of territorial to the organic system of functional representation. But it may at least be maintained, with some show of reason, that with that change, one of the most persistent obstacles to political efficiency will have been removed.

IDEA-REPRESENTATION

There will also be needed a second type of representation. This, too, must follow genuine rather than artificial lines of demarcation. It may be called "opinion-representation." Men differ not only in their basic occupational functions and in the interests and expertnesses which these basic functions generate; they differ also in their attitudes toward various social questions. There are, for example, individuals who believe in sumptuary control, and those who do not; there are those who believe in disarmament, or companionate marriage, or constitutional reform, and those who do not. At any particular time in the life of a people, some such conflict of opinions is in evidence; and individuals tend to range themselves in groups in support of their opinions. Hitherto, however, there has been no effective way in which such opinion-groups could function in the government of society. In America, for example, an individual can operate as a political citizen only by joining one of the parties. Since the minority parties are scarcely ever able to achieve representation, effective participation has meant voting for one of the two major parties. These, however, have represented such a medley of attitudes and policies—the two parties, in fact, being, for the most part, indistinguishable—that they have not served as the means whereby special groups of individuals, with special beliefs, could effectively operate. Thus minority opinions, such as socialism, or birth control, or constitutional reform, have had no way of gaining representation in governmental affairs, with the result that government has continued to be the expression of only a few major interests and points of view.

What evidently is needed is a kind of proportional representation which will give to every interest capable of winning a stipulated degree of support representation proportionate to its strength. This is altogether just and wise. It is just, since a genuine belief should have the right to a voice in government; it is wise, since an adequate government, representative of its people, will wish all possible points of view to be expressed within the halls of legislation in order that legislation may achieve comprehensiveness of wisdom.

We need, then, to visualize a second chamber elected, by proportional representation, on the basis of opinion-grouping. The voting for such representatives would indeed be by territorial districts, but the fact that the grouping would be by opinions or points of view, and the additional fact that in any district there would doubtless be a number of different opinion-groups, removes the objection raised above to territorial representation pure and simple. In other words, the lines of demarcation between groups would be genuine rather than artificial, and the individuals elected would, in all likelihood, be selected, in proportion to the strength of their groups, with far greater intelligence than is now evident under our present outgrown system.

When one visualizes the possibility of these two types

of representation—one by function and one by social idea—one realizes under what handicaps our traditional system has been operating. Our contemporary problem is not merely to elect good men; it is far more deeply the problem of so reorganizing the processes of government that good men will have a greater chance to be selected and to serve more effectively. The government of the past may have been good for the past; the government of the immediate future must be so organized as to correspond to the new realities that have entered into our life.

CHAPTER 12. TRANSCENDING POLITICAL LOYALTIES

IF, for the first time in its life, a child were to look down a railroad track, it would believe (provided its visual power were sufficiently developed) that the two lines of rail ran together. Later, it would learn to correct this sense-deception. It would then see one condition of affairs, but it would think another. It would be able to say to itself: "Tracks are not actually wider when they are near me, and narrower as they are farther away. Nearness to me makes no real difference. The tracks are equally wide at all distances."

In the realm of our senses, the "fallacy of perspective" is soon corrected. In the region of our feelings, however, it is not so easily escaped. Familiarity with things or persons near at hand tends to develop a kind of affection for them which, in turn, engenders an over-valuation. The fallacy begins at the point of one's own ego. One is to oneself the most vivid of existences. No one else can have quite the reality that one has for oneself. And so one is to oneself of primary importance. This feeling of vivid reality extends to one's belongings. One has a sense of their being something quite special in value, and one is concerned about them far more than about the belongings of others. This same feeling extends to one's close associates—first to mother and father, brothers and sisters, later to wife and children. One encircles these within a special area of affection and loyalty and regards them as of greater importance than mere acquaintances or strangers.

Doubtless this is all part of our essential psychological nature. We cannot ever hope to achieve a universality of outlook which will make us as sensitive to relationships that are distant as to those that are near. To love all men with the warmth with which one loves those who are near and dear seems to be a psychological impossibility. In other words, we shall always *feel* those who are close to us more vividly than those who are not close, just as we shall always *see* the near tracks as wider than the distant. A fallacy arises, however, when we mistake this immediacy of feeling for a superiority of value. If I believe that my children are better than other children because they are mine and I have a love for them, I merely translate my strength of feeling into an objective value. My children may be a good deal worse than other children. From the standpoint of true thinking, I ought to realize this and correct the false perspective. But in many cases the immediacy of feeling over-rides objective facts, and we disproportionately value "our own."

The more immature we are, the more closely we thus identify values with feelings. The small boy thinks his father is the best ever. Later he grows into the recognition that his father is an average individual. In so doing, he corrects the falsity of his childhood perspective. Thereafter, however intense his affection for the parent may be, he does not permit it to confuse his judgment. He learns, in other words, how to think straight at the same time that he feels warmly.

SOCIAL PERSPECTIVE

It is in their social relationships that most individuals are not fully matured. One frequently finds this to be the case in the loyalties of college young people to their fraternity fellows. One may grant a value to fraternities. That like-minded individuals should live together adds something both gracious and stimulating to life. But that these same like-minded individuals, as fraternity members, should exalt the value of their own fellows and assume a condescending attitude toward others, merely means that they are making an over-valuation in terms of nearness of relation. A like immaturity is exhibited in the prevailing type of college loyalty. Students and alumni usually attend debates and athletic contests not with minds set on objective values, but with emotions enlisted in uncritical support of their own particular group.

Loyalty to one's nation is frequently of a piece with these. Decatur's "my country, right or wrong" is obviously the declaration that the group-tie is superior to the truth-tie. Psychologically there is every reason why one should develop a warm affection for the land of one's birth and nurture. There is every reason, also, why one should like to be with those with whom one has lived the major portion of one's life. To be a stranger among strange folk is ever an uncomfortable condition. The language and the customs inhibit free and easy intercourse. There is little sharing of a common experience. One therefore feels out of place. If, now, one is immature of mind, one may translate one's discomfort into a condemnation of the folk among whom one's lot is cast. A wiser individual will not so distort the values. He will recognize that the source of the discomfort lies merely in the unfamiliarity, and he will refuse to be so foolish as to judge that these people who unwittingly make him unhappy are therefore inferior.

PATRIOTISM

Patriotism, in its usual form, is one of the most mischievous of our social immaturities. It is doubtless fated either to pass away or to be considerably modified. For we now sufficiently recognize that the love of a citizen for his nation is not an inborn characteristic nor one necessary to life. The Stoics visualized a commonwealth of man and man a citizen of the world. The Church of the Middle Ages was accorded a loyalty that transcended loyalty to a local government. It may quite easily be that loyalty-to-nation—which is, after all, a recent development among us—may yet pass into some other more essential type of loyalty.

For we now know that modern nations are not the sacred entities they have been made to appear to be. They came into being with the modern expansion of commercial enterprise, and they grew strong in the defense of it. They are, for the most part, simply more complex forms of earlier offensive and defensive organizations of corporate economic interests. When a contemporary nation goes to war, it does so, in practically all cases, for economic reasons. These reasons tend to be rationalized into high-sounding moralisms, like fighting for the nation's honor or fighting a war to end war. But when the psychological disguises are penetrated, national conflicts are almost invariably found to be conflicts of economic interests.

Recognizing this, we detect the absurdity of a loyalty that requires of us the abrogation of our judgment of values. Readiness to defend our country may simply mean readiness to defend economic interests that happen to have achieved commanding power. So the whole fabric of traditional patriotism begins to ravel. If we are to be loyal, let it be to something worthy of our loyalty.

REDUCTIO AD ABSURDUM

Traditionally our loyalties have been to territories and to the romanticized events which have taken place within them. Our efforts of loyalty have expended themselves in defense of these territories or in the expansion of them by military means. They have, in short, divided up the world in checkerboard fashion. They have built walls around special pieces of territory and have excluded all who did not live within these special pieces. These other individuals might, in all essential respects, be exactly as high-minded as those who lived within the walls, but the fact that their loyalty was to another piece of earth and to the inhabitants thereof, made them potential or actual enemies.

Indeed a curious paradox has developed. A loyalty of this territorial kind inevitably must conflict with other loyalties of the same kind. Although each is good in itself, each is regarded by the others as bad. Thus the loyalty of a German to his country is a potentially bad thing for a Frenchman, while the Frenchman's loyalty to his France is a potentially bad thing for the German. And yet for each, the principle of loyalty to one's land is a good. How can that which is supposed to be intrinsically good turn out to be bad?

There is a fundamental contradiction in this kind of loyalty. A genuine moral principle excludes no one. If the principle is enunciated: "Love thy neighbor as thyself," the mark of its genuineness as a moral principle lies in the fact that it admits everyone who sincerely wishes to practice the principle. But suppose it were to read: "Love all thy neighbors who live within ten square miles and who are blondes." It would then cease to be a genuine moral principle!

Now it is because territorial loyalty is the special privilege of a few that it is not a genuine moral principle. It may, indeed, be a principle of social expediency. For there are conditions under which it may be wise for individuals to band together to carry on their interests. They can do this, for example, for economic reasons, by forming a partnership or a corporation. Or they can do it for social reasons, by forming a bridge club or a hockey team. In each case they band together, and they naturally exclude a great many other individuals. But no one in his senses would call loyalty to such a group the highest obligation of the members. This, however, is precisely what we expect of the members of a territorial group. Because one happens to have been born in a certain country, one must consider one's obligation to that particular territory and to the inhabitants thereof as higher than all other obligations in the world.

The *reductio ad absurdum* of the principle of territorial loyalty is found in certain post-war happenings in Europe. There bewildered individuals have been bandied about from one nationality to another. Up in the Tyrolean mountains, good, law-abiding Germans are compelled now to be Italian. They have had no traditional interest in the governmental organization called Italy. But the Italian walls having been forcibly thrown around them, they are now expected to reorientate their feelings and become ardently attached to this their new fatherland.

FROM SPURIOUS TO GENUINE PATRIOTISM

We are seriously questioning all this curious business of "walling in or walling out." As Robert Frost expresses it:

> "*Before I built a wall I'd ask to know*
> *What I was walling in or walling out,*
> *And to whom I was like to give offence.*
> *Something there is that doesn't love a wall,*
> *That wants it down.*"

A new kind of loyalty is emerging—one with walls down. It is a loyalty not to special territories but to truth. Truth never excludes. The truth that the Frenchman, Pasteur, finds is equally good and equally true for a German. The truth of insight that a Beethoven finds is equally a truth for his territorial enemies across the Rhine. Indeed, when we contemplate the majesty of the great truths of science, art, and the good life, the separative loyalties to special territories seem not only petty but malignant.

CONTRIBUTORY PATRIOTISM

Let us put the issue sharply by asking what kind of loyalty to one's land one should expect of oneself and others. Hitherto the loyalty-concept has been bound up with readiness to defend. The image of the world has been that of an especially dear territory surrounded by potential or actual enemies. It is this deeply graven image that has played havoc in the past and that still plays havoc in the present. It has led each individual to believe that the most essential quality of his land was its defensibility, its power to resist, and, if necessary, its power to overcome. The concept has been essentially a military one. One's fatherland has been one's *powerland*. Thus the British choose for one of their national anthems the line: "Britannia rules the waves." Our own "Star Spangled Banner" is an ecstasy over "bombs bursting in air."

All this belongs to a past that is rapidly being left behind. An interweaving of interests throughout the world has made the mutual isolation of territories no longer possible save with disaster. The rise of the creative universalism of science has brought to each nation a wealth of insight that belongs with equal right to all the other nations. Chinese walls are ineffectual against the overmastering sweep of truths that unite all men.

Thus we must either find for ourselves a new basis of

patriotism, or declare that this sentiment is too low and divisive for intelligent modern human beings.

Suppose one were to ask oneself this question: "Why should I be proud of my country, willing to work for it, and, if necessary, to defend it?" The answer can no longer be: "I am proud of my country because she is able to rule the waves; I am willing to defend my country because other countries are inferior to mine and threaten her existence." All this is infantile, and goes out with the bag and baggage of our other infantilisms. But one might quite properly answer in some such way as this: "I am proud of my country because of the great contributions its institutions and citizens have made to the rest of the world. I am willing to work for the continuance of that kind of contribution to the world. And I am willing to defend the institutions of my country and the citizens of my country against any danger, either within or without, that threatens the continuance of this power to contribute to the betterment of the world."

Suppose that one were an Englishman. One might quite properly say: "I am proud to belong to the country that produced Magna Charta, that gave scope to the genius of Shakespeare, that produced a Newton and a Darwin." If one were an Englishman, one might equally say: "I share the pride of the German in his Goethe and his Kant; I share the pride of the Frenchman in his Rousseau and Pasteur and Madame Curie; I share the pride of the Hindu in his Mahabarata and Gautama and Tagore." Such proud loyalty to one's own land becomes, then, not a principle which excludes but one which includes. It becomes not a special privilege for oneself and one's fellow landsmen; it becomes a privilege which one shares with all.

In short, the only kind of patriotism which can continue on into a saner world is *contributory patriotism.* Such patriotism builds for itself a different kind of image. No longer of a special territory in a surrounding world of enemies, the image is now of a group of people surrounded by other groups, all of them essentially human and all of them seeking, by mutual interchange of what is true, good, and beautiful, to carry on with an increasing success this strange adventure of life.

THE NEW OBLIGATION

When, then, is one patriotic in the genuine sense of this word? The answer is: when one defends or advances the contributory powers of one's country. This will require something quite different from a readiness to defend with musket or poison gas. It will require a willingness to be alert to all the forces that threaten the contributory powers that struggle to expression in one's midst. Thus it will be patriotic to oppose the stirrers-up of mass passion against other people; it will be patriotic to take action against those who, in novel or play or film or newspaper, arouse prejudice by flagrant misrepresentations; it will be patriotic to work against those in one's own land or elsewhere who exploit the lives of the defenseless for their own selfish purposes. There will, in short, be the obligation to defend life-values against those who seek to destroy them. But it will be patriotic, too, to make disinterested research in laboratories, to invent, to write books, to compose music, to organize wholesome recreation.

Genuine patriotism, in short, will consist in all those attitudes and activities that defend and support universally shareable values.

From this point of view, the patriotism that can hound a Kreisler during wartime, or cast out the language and literature of a great people from the schools and colleges because that language and literature happen to belong to the enemy, has its place on a sub-civilized level of life. In future, many more of us may be willing to go to prison rather than have commerce with that species of pernicious provincialism. Contributory patriotism is cast in more generous mold. It is a loyalty to those great shareable values that both support and overarch the processes and groupings of our life and that give us the only justification for regarding the human race as of any significance whatever. It was of such loyalty that Euripides was doubtless thinking when he wrote: "Every land is fatherland to noble men." [1]

[1] Fragments, 1047.

PART III

WAYS AHEAD

"These are the spells by which to reassume
An empire o'er the disentangled doom."
SHELLEY—*Prometheus Unbound*

CHAPTER 13. THE GREAT TOLERANCES

THE civilization with which we are familiar has, for a number of centuries, been characterized by four major intolerances. Intolerance, therefore, has been of the very fibre of our being. This is so startling a thought that it calls for careful elaboration.

INSTITUTIONALIZED RELIGION

The first of our persistent intolerances has been generated by institutionalized religion. We find that, during the past centuries, the average Christian has simply taken his religion for granted as paramount in value, assuming that other religions were inferior to his. He has regretted the misfortune of individuals who did not have the opportunity to be born or converted into his own particular belief. He has wished them well; but he has had his doubts about the cultural and spiritual level that could be attained by anyone not blessed as he was with cosmic assurance. Substitute here for "the average Christian," "the average Mohammedan," or "the average Jew," or "the average Hindu," and the situation remains unaltered.

Religion, in brief, has belonged not to the region of matters to be quietly reasoned about, compared as to relative merits, and experimented with, but to the region of what is fully, finally, and exclusively accepted; to the region of the axiomatic, of the "what-every-person-of-my kind-knows-is-true." Hence in their religious life people have, for the most part, been contented dogmatists.

Even where the religion has been substantially the same, people have divided themselves into their special areas of dogmatic certitude and superiority. In Christian lands, they have occupied Baptist or Methodist or Episcopalian areas, and they have thanked their common God that He belonged to them a little more truly and intimately than to their neighbors. "Love your neighbor as yourself" has been subtly transformed into: "Pity your neighbor, even have a little contempt for him, because he is not as religiously enlightened as you yourself."

I remember standing on a street corner in a small town in a middle western state and suddenly awakening to the fact that, with five stones in my hand, I could, if I wished, have easily hit five churches. Religion in that small town —so small that it could hardly have supported one church —was obviously not a uniting but a dividing factor, segregating its inhabitants into five areas of more or less mutual intolerance.

To be sure, difference of view is not in itself an evil. Indeed, it is essential to mental and spiritual progress. Thus scientists and scholars differ among themselves. But the attitude which they hold toward their differences is singularly other than that which has characterized differing religionists. Among the former, there is always the assumption that the differences are open to friendly inspection and discussion. Among religionists, the typical assumption has been that of having secure possession of the exclusive truth, so that friendly discussion, with the possibility of mutual modification, has been severely ruled out.

The difference is a peculiarly subtle one, but of very essential importance as we move into modern ways of thought and behavior. Perhaps the most significant aspect of our modern attitude is the rejection of absolutes. Religion, for the most part, was born in ages when the absolutistic attitude was the prevailing one. There was absolutism in morals, in political organization, in social relationships. The modern age has dissolved most of these absolutes. Thus, in morals, we now begin to adopt an evolutionary attitude, believing that morals inevitably alter as the conditions of life change. So likewise in political organization and social relationships, we begin to accept the fact that no past order of life is exempted from the necessity of undergoing modification. Religion has been the last to feel the impact of this evolutionary point of view. While there have been individual religionists who have accepted the fact that religion, like everything else, grows with the growth of the world, the absolutistic attitude has largely prevailed, so that religious adherents have held to their beliefs in the old spirit of an unquestioning loyalty to something that is beyond doubt and without shadow of change.

This type of religious self-assurance has been so bred in the bone of most people, even of the present generation, that they have scarcely given it a thought. They have received it, as it were, as a child receives its mother's milk, and they have grown into a kind of lustiness of intolerant maturity without even wondering whether they ought not to be ashamed of it and learn to mend their ways. Thus the Hindu quietly, and with complete self-congratulation, pities those who are not of his own religion; the Mohammedan and the Christian, with the same complete self-congratulation, though a little less quietly, do likewise. Each thanks his special God that he is not as these others.

NATIONALISM

There is a second intolerance into which we have been born—that generated by nationhood. From childhood days people are taught to be proud of the fact that they belong to the particular nation that is theirs. In school, teachers strive conscientiously to develop "good citizenship," which invariably means, among other things, that individuals are to hold themselves in readiness to defend and to propagate the particular culture which is their nation's. These teachers do not ask their young charges to consider whether other nations may not have more to offer to the world than their own. They are easily helped in their indoctrination of a special culture by the tales they assign their pupils to read about the glories of their own nation's achievements and the impeccable virtues of its heroes.

Quite deliberately, in short, people all over the world are educated into a special admiration and a special loyalty; and almost before they know it, they are content to believe that a kindly Providence made them Englishmen, or Frenchmen, or Germans, as the case may be.

"For he might have been a Roosian,
A French, or Turk or Proosian,
Or perhaps Itali-an!
But, in spite of all temptations,
To belong to other nations,
He remains an Englishman." [1]

Few of us have been given to contemplating the contradictory logic involved in a world where each group fervently believes itself to be the best. When an intolerance comes in by the door, a somewhat bewildered logic flies out by the window.

ECONOMIC INTOLERANCE

A third intolerance is generated by our habitual acceptance of the kind of economic order in which we live. Aristotle was quite ready to believe that slaves were necessary in a properly ordered world. He did not spend his sympathies in contemplation of the sad fate of hundreds of thousands of his less fortunate fellows. He was wrapped in a kind of spiritual cellophane, which kept his sympathies untouched by anything that lay outside the region of his accepted economic belief. The same is true in any established economic order. The feudal aristocrat took it for granted, without thinking about it, that the rulership of the bloodworthy was the only acceptable way of life. The modern entrepreneur has taken it for granted that economic enterprise must be carried on by the hiring and fir-

[1] Sir W. S. Gilbert, *Pinafore.*

ing of "the hewers of wood and the drawers of water."

Wherever, in short, a particular economic pattern has prevailed, critical thinking in respect to its value and permanence has, in large measure, been estopped. The pattern has had the right of way. It has taken unto itself a kind of inviolability, and it has generated an intolerance of any system other than its own. In the present day, we know well enough how this type of intolerance has ruled our life. The very thought of putting heads together and trying to think a way through to a system of life possibly quite different from that to which we have grown accustomed has aroused a kind of righteous horror. Criticisms of the prevailing system have been met, for the most part, not by intellectual generosity, but by emotional resistance. If other systems are tried elsewhere, they are not calmly evaluated; they are judged to be something unworthy of full and free discussion.

RACE

Perhaps the deepest and the darkest of our intolerances is that of race. The Nordic has had a sense of God-given obligation. He has felt that he was appointed to bear the white man's burden. If he has chanced to be more than usually imaginative, he may well have conceived the Lord on high considering His various handiwork, shaking His head a little ruefully over Mongolians, Semitics, Ethiopians. He, the Lord God, made them, indeed; but He feels sorry He made them. They were a kind of mistake. But His face brightens. He has his Nordics. They will help Him—those very satisfying children of His, with their shining white faces and eager unselfishness. They will go forth in His name, and Mongolians, Semitics, and Ethiopians will be made into something a little less offensive to His divine self-respect.

The story repeats itself all over the world. The very Semitic whom the Nordic has despised has despised the Nordic. Did not God discipline him, the Semitic, for a special mission? Did He not give him the authentic word? Did He not ordain him to obliterate whole cities of the unelect, lest the word spoken to Abraham and Isaac should be mispronounced or misapplied?

The Mongolian has smiled his enigmatic smile. Vulgar upstarts, he has thought, contemplating the Western folk; creatures without courtesy, without grace, without beauty or reverence, making loud noises in the world, vaunting their ignorant absolutes, covering their hypocrisies with cloaks of piety. Best let them alone in their underbred violences. A pebble falls into the eternal ocean, and the ocean does not ask: "What has hurt me?"

Meanwhile, among them all the Ethiopian has looked on wistfully, wondering about the queer world into which he has been cast, bending his neck submissively to the yoke imposed by his superiors, cherishing in his heart a dream of a land where angels sing sweetly and a mighty, loving God gives comfort to the sufferer.

It has been an ugly thing, this racial intolerance. It, too, has been bred in the bone of us, so that today, if we are Nazis, we take pride in beating a Jew, or if we are a certain type of American, we railroad black men to the death house. To each, in short, there has been a pride of race that has sustained him in his righteous hatreds and that has given him his sense of being an especially privileged co-worker with God.

NEW ATTITUDES

Four intolerances—and a new civilization in the making! If anything far-reaching is to be accomplished in the future, these major intolerances must be done away with. They have bred in us a quality of mind that has in large degree hindered the development of more authentic values and that has made our religious, political, economic, and racial life one of continuing mutual animosity.

Can a different quality of mind be bred? Are there signs that this new quality is taking shape among us? Are there any indications where it is emerging into being?

It may be said with some degree of hopefulness that in all four regions of our life there is a growing movement away from the habitual intolerances. Thus, in religion, one finds an increasing distaste for the kind of missionarizing in which one religious culture attempts outright to supplant another. Modern thought begins to accept the fact that all peoples, in one way or another, have discovered spiritual truth; and the missionary of today is far more likely to be zealous in finding and preserving the good that is contained in a religious culture foreign to his own than in exterminating it root and branch. Indeed, we are far more likely nowadays to believe that

> *"One accent of the Holy Ghost*
> *The heedless world hath never lost;"*

in short, that greatness of spiritual insight has not been vouchsafed to one people only, or to one prophet or group of prophets, but to all peoples in all times. There is a growing tendency to think of a Bible of Humanity as consisting of all the spiritual insights which have been achieved by man in his long and various history.

Likewise in the regions of nationalistic thinking, a breaking up of the traditional intolerances is increasingly in evidence. Methods of teaching history are being severely criticised in so far as they have lent themselves to nationalistic propaganda and to the breeding of prejudiced attitudes toward other nations and peoples. Indeed, there is a widespread tendency among the scholars in this field to advance the study of history to world dimensions, so that the major emphasis will be placed on the interrelationships of nations and peoples rather than upon a purely national exclusiveness. And finally there is a movement among all the advanced nations of the world—feeble as yet, no doubt, but growing—to consider seriously an entrance into a new order of political life, more reasonable and more generous, in which political divisions will serve as convenient administrative boundaries rather than as indicators of exclusive loyalties and mutual antagonisms.

In economic life, we are all well enough aware of the unprecedented degree to which a new tolerance in regard to unaccustomed views has begun to develop. In this case necessity has been the mother of broadening minds, but it is a good omen that the broadening has actually been taking place. While there will, no doubt, be periodic returns to a habit of economic intolerance, we are fortunately at a point in our history where, for the time being, an openness to views hitherto unfamiliar and a willingness to examine them with some degree of dispassionateness begins to be in evidence.

New economic fanaticisms have been born, to be sure. The intolerance of the stand-patter now takes second place before the intolerance of the radical. Whether this type of intolerance will play new havoc with our life depends upon the degree to which we can develop the habit of critical consideration of the economic forms and forces of our life. In any event, we are moving out of the unquestioning acceptance of old theories and ways of economic existence.

Finally, in the region of racial prejudice—the worst of all—there seems to be a considerable movement toward more generous attitudes. Even at best, the road ahead is not an easy one, for racial differences have a curious way of involving the emotional life to an extent not found where the differences are those of status or occupation or mentality. Nevertheless the modern world shows signs of a growing distaste for those undiscriminating condemnations which are visited upon individuals solely on the ground of their racial connections. Doubtless a new sense of basic justice is developing among us, which estimates individuals in terms of intrinsic qualities of worth rather than in terms of extrinsic qualities due to the accident of birth.

Hence, in these four regions, where intolerance has been typical, new attitudes are evidently developing, making it not impossible to believe that the coming civilization will move along lines more generous than those along which the civilizations of the past have gone their way.

OTHER FORCES CONTRIBUTE

Meanwhile, it is worth noting that there are current tendencies which powerfully contribute to this advance toward more hospitable ways of existence. These tendencies are not wholly new. All through history, in fact, there has been a kind of golden stream of great tolerances. This stream has been growing more powerful as our civilization has advanced, and today it may be said to be one of the chief forces which is sweeping away the old landmarks of intolerance.

Throughout the centuries, for example, there has been manifest now and again the tolerance of the "two or three gathered together." Socrates sought out others that he might learn of them and with them. He made no pretensions to the possession of truth. He sincerely sought for something that he could not find wholly within himself. He talked with these others, and through the dialectic of discussion, he helped to make a new clarity emerge.

This is a pattern of behavior which, whenever it appears among men, manifests itself as genuine. It overrides artificial classifications. Socrates could talk as easily and as understandingly with a slave boy as with a citizen, with the poor as with the rich. And one would suppose that if he were living in this day of many sects, parties, and races, he would talk as easily with a Hindu as with a Baptist, with a negro as with a white, with a Jew as with a Gentile, with a conservative Republican as with a liberal Democrat.

Is there, in our modern life, any evidence of this Socratic spirit of putting heads together? We have one outstanding example of its effectiveness in the rebirth of a whole people through its peculiarly modern use. Bishop Grundtvig, whom we have already mentioned, was a kind of Danish Socrates who taught the young men and women of his land this art of coming together, talking things over, and clarifying their ideas and life-objectives through the tolerant give-and-take of discussion.

In our own land, we find this way of life manifest in those gatherings of people in which the coming together is in the spirit of complete tolerance; where Jew and Gentile are equally welcome, where Catholic can sit next to Methodist, and Methodist next to atheist; where the rich have no more rights than the poor, and where even the black man has his welcome. In innumerable communities throughout the land such gatherings for the discussion of matters pertinent to the search for social good take place. Sometimes they meet in a Jewish synagogue or in a Christian church, sometimes in a school auditorium, sometimes in a town hall. Wherever they take place, the ordinary barriers to free and generous intercourse are removed. The customary rules of our highly compartmentalized life are suspended, and men talk freely with their fellows.

For the most part, perhaps, these meetings are fumbling affairs. They do not reach glittering conclusions. And those who have talked—or listened—frequently go away in a mood of exasperation. All this, no doubt, is due to the immaturity of our social intelligence. We have not yet learned to meet together with an easy and gracious effectiveness. Our individualities rasp; our crude blunderings antagonize. The suspicions born of immemorial prejudices follow us even into these halls of generous togetherness.

But, despite it all, something deeply authentic seems to occur in these gatherings. For the time being, at least, walls are down, and while Pallas Athene may not rise full-panoplied out of those headaches of talk, a kind of new wisdom is being born—that of a common seeking for a common good.

THE TOLERANCE OF HELP

Two thousand years ago we had the figure of the great Helper. We have had that figure in many lands and times. He heals the sick, comforts the oppressed. He makes no distinctions of class or race or monetary status. He is as likely to help the "certain man" fallen among thieves as the rich man's daughter who is at death's door. Wherever he appears, he manifests what is genuine in life.

Is there, in our contemporary society, any evidence of this spirit? It will be found, one suspects, wherever the aiding of the unfortunate is given wholly in the spirit of help and without reference to creed, politics, citizenship, or race. Even today it is difficult to find this transcendence of all the customary lines of demarcation. But there are strong movements in this direction. Most significant, perhaps, is the movement toward the complete communalizing of help. The Community Chest is increasingly like the Ark of the Covenant in the Temple: it belongs not to one sect or set within the temple of the community but to all. The Red Cross was conceived in such a spirit of complete disregard of the ordinary lines of division. There are times, indeed, when passionate exclusivenesses override this more genuine spirit—as in military and industrial war—but the pressure of what is authentic in that spirit grows stronger, and it is not unreasonable to suppose that the time is approaching when neither patriotism nor economic bitternesses will invade the spirit of helping where help is needed. We are hoping that the days of charity will eventually be past; but as long as the world is as badly maladjusted as it is, the spirit of charitable help will be needed. As long as charity does not become a kind of self-justification for forgetting the graver issues of social reconstruction, it remains a spiritual asset.

This spirit of the helper is perhaps most broadly exemplified in our contemporary days in the life of an individual like Jane Addams. In Hull House we find an institution consciously dedicated to a complete and unhesitant identification with the common lot. When one moves within the generous atmosphere of that place of sanctuary, the ordinary divisions of class, race, fortune, and nation seem not only out of keeping with the spirit of our humanity but a kind of desecration of what human life has it in it to be.

SCIENTISTS

In contemporary days, when reputations are being blown away like dried leaves in a wind, there is one area of life which has remained unaffected by the strong blasts of our disillusionment. It is the area of the scientist. Here, however fumbling and tentative the results may be, we recognize the motivation as genuine. We find lives dedicated to an authentic enterprise. And wherever we discover this particular enterprise being carried on by individual or group with the disinterestedness that is both the pride and the power of science, we know ourselves to be in the presence of something that will endure.

Whatever the new order of life is to be, then, it is coming to birth wherever the rigorously equipped and rigorously honest mind of a scientist is at work. That, no doubt, is why the figure of an Einstein is so dramatically impressive today. A Jew, he belongs to the area of our inherited persecutional complexes; a German, he should have visited upon him the bitterness of narrow nationalisms; a pacifist, he should be the object of militaristic hatreds. And yet, despite attacks, he remains among us serenely impervious, because, in the best sense of that word, he is a man of science. However we ourselves mishandle life, we give our confidence to those whose devotion is to scientific exploration. Wherever we find such devotion selling its heritage for a mess of commercial pottage, we grieve that the mighty are fallen—which indicates clearly enough that in our own estimation the kingdom of the new is to be born where devotions are selfless, where, in brief, there is a yielding of one's powers and interests to an enterprise greater than oneself. Because we find this kind of selflessness exemplified in the true scientist, we may take it for granted that wherever the spirit of science is operative, we are in the presence of that which belongs to the new order of life.

CREATORS

Perhaps the most striking exemplification of what man has it in him to be is found in those instances in which he makes a selective approach to life and creates significant experience. Every artist does this. He is not a mere acceptor of life as it is. Nor is he one who, for his own uses, deliberately despoils life. On the contrary, he creates out of the relatively unordered materials of existence an experience that has an arresting loveliness. He thereby adds to the worth of life. We note this in a Euripides, a Phidias, a Leonardo. Each of these enlarges the range of our experience so that it takes on new meaning. We note this also in the philosophers. They, too, through their interpretative wonderings, create new experiences for us, that widen the scope and intensify the quality of our life.

Among such creators there is no fundamental intolerance. A Leonardo can have respect for an Aristotle, as an Aristotle, no doubt, could have respect for a Phidias. Among lesser artists and philosophers, indeed, there is evident at times a petty inhospitality, but precisely in the degree that these individuals are lesser. The spirit of the genuine artist and philosopher is that of creating in beauty and meaning, and where that spirit prevails, life attains a level of true achievement.

PLAY

Finally, there is play. In all times it has been one of man's most delightful behaviors. In its very essence, play is generous. Even where it is competitive, it is usually without rancor. Where there is defeat of an adversary, the defeat involves no tragedy. Play is a friendly coming-together in mutually enjoyable activity.

No doubt the fine flower of play is the spirit of good sportsmanship, the one ethical quality that never smacks of sentimentality or smugness. It is essentially the quality of decent fellowship, the spirit of the individual respecting both himself and others.

In the newspapers, as I write, there are accounts of the trial in Russia of six Englishmen charged with espionage and the attempt to wreck major industrial plants in the Soviet Union. Whether the charges are true or not, we feel that they might quite easily be true. This is precisely the kind of ugly behavior that one expects in business and between nations. In these regions one does not look for good sportsmanship. One looks for ugliness because all's fair in war and business. Out of it no true new civilization can be born.

It is significant that in play, for the most part, the ordinary barriers of race, social status, sex, nationality, politics and religion are removed. One of the outstanding signs of something new being born among us is the complete openness—nationally, racially, religiously—of such a play-enterprise as the Olympic Games. In the midst of an intensity of competitiveness that, with all the unseemliness of chicanery, propaganda, espionage and sabotage, might have ranged nation against nation, these international games, despite all their shortcomings, have been carried on in the spirit of decent human beings doing their best to win but for the most part taking their defeat like good sportsmen.

In thousands of places throughout the land, every day of the year, this good sportsmanship of play is in evidence. It may be said to be building in us a new kind of integrity—that of generous participation in an enterprise in which even defeat can be a kind of triumph, the triumph of having played one's part to the best of one's ability and of having met a new challenge to one's powers.

CONCLUSION

Here, then, in the coöperative enterprise of putting heads together, in the lending of help regardless of distinctions of rank, religion, or race, in the rigorous pursuit of scientific truth, in the creating of beauty and meaning, in the good sportsmanship of play are additional forces in our contemporary life that are powerfully carrying us in a direction away from the historic intolerances. There is every reason, in short, to suppose that the movement of life is toward a widening of areas and a more willing participation in a common human destiny.

CHAPTER 14. NEW USES OF FREEDOM

WE are passing out of a work-bound world into one of growing freedom. Indeed, as opportunities for liberation from traditional drudgeries increase, we find people voicing a new kind of declaration of independence.

> "*What is this life if, full of care,*
> *We have no time to stand and stare.*
>
> *No time to stand beneath the boughs*
> *And stare as long as sheep or cows.*
>
> *No time to see, when woods we pass,*
> *Where squirrels hide their nuts in grass.*
>
> *No time to see, in broad daylight,*
> *Streams full of stars, like skies at night.*
>
> *No time to turn at Beauty's glance,*
> *And watch her feet, how they can dance.*
>
> *No time to wait till her mouth can*
> *Enrich that smile her eyes began.*

A poor life this if, full of care,
We have no time to stand and stare."[1]

There is, too, a growing sense of pity for those whose enslavement is so great that the more fascinating opportunities of existence are denied them.

"Let not young souls be smothered out before
They do quaint deeds and fully flaunt their pride.
It is the world's one crime its babes grow dull,
Its poor are ox-like, limp and leaden-eyed.

"Not that they starve, but starve so dreamlessly,
Not that they sow, but that they seldom reap,
Not that they serve, but have no gods to serve,
Not that they die but that they die like sheep."[2]

We are indeed witnessing the movement of a whole society into a way of life that hitherto has been reserved for a special privileged class. In the past, the leisure class was sharply set off from the rest of society. The privileges of its members were unique, and it was presumed that individuals outside this class would do no more than envy their more fortunate fellows. These leisured individuals, born, so to speak, with worklessness as their portion, developed arts of life consistent with their apartness from the rough labors of the world. They developed elegances of manner, nice trivialities of behavior, polite gaieties to wile

[1] W. H. Davies: *Leisure;* from *Collected Poems;* by permission of Jonathan Cape and Harrison Smith, publishers.

[2] Vachel Lindsay: *The Leaden-Eyed;* from *Collected Poems;* by permission of The Macmillan Company, publishers.

away empty hours. In order to maintain the vigor of their bodies, they pursued military exercises and the hunt. In order to preserve the vigor of their minds, they engaged in the clever duplicities of statecraft and the nice extravagances of literary discourse. The fine flower of such privileged leisure was found in a Plato, a Leonardo, a Sir Walter Raleigh. The common garden variety was found in the pompous braggart, the fripperied fop, the poetic despoiler of virgins, the roystering gamester, the bored futilitarian.

The new movement of leisure has its birth in the soil of significant work. It is not unlikely, then, that the forms which our leisure is to take will possess qualities very different from those with which we have hitherto been familiar. Thus the Platos of a modern world will be spectators and interpreters of a range of existence withheld from their highborn forerunners. Plato, for example, had no concern with the fate of slaves. A modern philosopher, born into the democratic atmosphere of a world in which work is the common portion, will include all areas of life in his survey. The same will be true of the Leonardos and Sir Walter Raleighs of today. Philosophy, literature, art, in other words, will inevitably shape themselves in response to a world of wider relationships and more inclusive destiny. The same will be true of statecraft and the military skills. They will take on new forms in terms of attitudes that spring out of a workaday sense of common contribution rather than out of the aristocratic sense of privileged appropriation. The same transformation of quality will take place in the more ordinary pleasures. The average aristocrat of former centuries, with all time at his disposal, would quite naturally develop a taste for pleasures different from those sought by an average modern individual whose pleasure-time is a brief resting between periods of labor. He would in all likelihood be a connoisseur of the rare, the exotic, the subtle. The brief rester is far more likely to have a greater zest for the less subtle, a heartier enjoyment of that which is obtained at a minimum cost of preparation and pursuit. For even when he has time to "stand and stare," he will be conscious of the passing of the time, and he will be likely to snatch what he can with a swiftness that makes impossible the development of a fine discrimination of taste and appreciation.

Thus with the passing of a privileged class there is due to take place a very considerable transformation of leisure pursuits and of the qualities of mind and attitude bred by the opportunities of leisure. Such a transformation is now taking place among us. An old world of leisure is passing. What the new is to be is as yet scarcely predictable. But inasmuch as leisure has shaped much of what has been significant in human life, it is important that contemporary society should confront its growing opportunities with an intelligent awareness of what these opportunities promise of good and ill.

THE LEISURE OF ESCAPE

Naturally the first kind of leisure activity to be widely developed in a work-world is the leisure of escape. Such is the leisure one enjoys as a way of release from the hard demands of a utilitarian existence. The pleasure one seeks is something very different from one's day-by-day activities, something calculated to make one forget. The pursuit of it is therefore as far removed as possible from that concentrated application of one's energies which is demanded in the strenuous and ofttimes precarious effort to meet the challenge of life necessities.

In the meeting of this challenge, man has achieved a certain dignity, the dignity of a kind of valiant enlistment of his powers in the conquest of difficulties. It is with this in mind that Alvin Johnson draws the contrast between modern man the producer and modern man the consumer:

"Man as producer is often sublime; man as consumer is usually ridiculous. . . . In production we employ our best intelligence and the best of our will power. We adapt all our means purposefully to the ends we wish to attain. We are direct, honest, brave. Our productive function performed, we doff all these qualities and proceed to consume gluttonously, wastefully, irrationally, with a silly, dishonest eye to show and prestige.

". . . Here is a man whose intelligence dominates a mighty industry. A hundred thousand men do his bidding unquestioningly. In his office he is a king—better, a philosopher-king. Away from his office, all he can think of to pass the time is to pursue a gutta-percha ball around the green, wailing like a child if he happens to plant it in the rough. Here is a whole population of men and women of the more intelligent class—men who dominate the law, business, politics, women who dominate society and for whom more than for any other class pictures are painted, books are written, music is composed and performed. Look at them, in their leisure time desperately intent upon the chance composition of a hand of cards, to the exclusion of humor, wit, sense, spirit, and all the other proper elements of civilized social intercourse."[3]

The widespread leisure of mere escape indicates that no adequate adjustment has yet been made to the fact that we really can have leisure and can make something truly important out of it. It shows life come suddenly and unprepared upon a breathing space. Hitherto breathing spaces have been few and far between. We have not yet accustomed ourselves to the new fact that breathing spaces are being multiplied and prolonged and that we increasingly find ourselves with more and more opportunity to utilize "times off." So, with the old nervous haste of driven creatures, we tend to seek the easiest ways of enjoyment. We relinquish our major interests and take our swift excursions into a kind of forgetfulness. In doing so, we dissociate ourselves from ourselves. We make ourselves into dual creatures—significant in one aspect and contributory to the common lot; insignificant in another and merely appropriative of individual gratification.

Note the vast development of this art of forgetting in our contemporary society. The major portion of our literature is escape literature: the detective and romantic novel, the average short story, the scandal sheet. Each of these is a means of getting away from that which is significant, a

[3] Alvin Johnson; *Youth and Human Conservation;* in *Civilization and Enjoyments,* page 35; edited by Baker Brownell. Courtesy of D. Van Nostrand Company, publishers.

finding of release in a kind of other-world where obligations are no longer insistent and values cease to trouble. The major portion of our dramatic art is of like kind: the sentimental or adventurous photoplay, innocent of ideas and demanding on the part of the spectator no least stirring of the brain; vaudeville and musical comedy, riots of noise and movement, that titillate the eye and the ear, but leave the essential self untouched; the average stage play, repeating old patterns of life, and serving only to hold the spectator in a kind of excited suspense that successfully removes him from his ordinary concerns. The major sports likewise serve in large measure the function of escape. They are spectacles that we watch, letting ourselves go for the moment in the contemplation of enterprises not our own. To be sure, there are those who watch but who also play. Of these it may be said that the enjoyment of the spectacle is an extension of activities that they themselves have found worth while. But there are all too many for whom the spectacle is the only way of enjoyment and who develop the lesser art of merely looking on.

Dr. J. B. Nash, in a recent book,[4] has dubbed this kind of vicarious enjoyment "spectatoritis." This is the disease of individuals who have not yet achieved the vigor of mentality nor the nicety of taste to make of their leisure time something creatively significant and who seek the services of performers to help them achieve, effortlessly, a momentary abandonment of their world.

One must not, of course, be undiscriminating in one's analysis. There may be a value in pushing a gutta-percha

[4] *Spectatoritis;* Sears, New York City.

ball across a green or watching a baseball game or reading a detective novel, provided it is not the sole way in which the individual is able to spend his leisure time. What seems unfortunate, when we contemplate the escape ways of leisure, is that they are too frequently the only ways available to many individuals, so that the more valuable opportunities that lie within free time are lost. Also they are the ways most exploited by our commercial agencies, so that they tend, through the line of least resistance, to be most largely in evidence in our contemporary life.

LEISURE OF FULFILLMENT

Beyond the leisure of escape is the leisure of fulfillment. It has taken many forms in the past and it is doubtless destined to play an increasing part in the future. This leisure involves activities that in one way or another have intrinsic value in the life of the individual.

Thus, hard-pressed with labor as people may have been, there have always been those who have managed to take time out for some activity that added something to the value of their life—the playing of a musical instrument, or singing; attempts at family orchestras; an hour snatched for some fine reading; twilight time spent in planting a garden; a walk in the woods; or the pursuit of some special hobby, like woodcarving or collecting old prints. In every such case, brief as the leisure time may have been, it has been so occupied as to supplement the regular life-activities with something of value. Into these leisure activities, the individual has carried his own self, and while he has not been able to build these precious snatches of experience into a rounded whole of life, he has found himself steadied and enlarged by them.

In other cases, especially in rural regions, leisure time has been occupied in such a way as to fit the person into a broader pattern of life. In the folk dance, the husking bee, the old-fashioned spelling match, the "sociable," the individual emerged for a while from his work-life to participate in a social play-life. In these social activities, to be sure, he momentarily forgot the demand of his daily work, but through them he moved into an order of life that was essentially part of his work-life, so that he merely expanded his workaday self into its broader relationships.

Perhaps one of the regrettable features of the individualism that has followed in the train of city life is that this type of self-fulfillment through the group is hardly any longer in evidence. Individuals are cast back upon themselves, to find through their own separate pursuits such supplementation of their activities as is within their power. Doubtless there is grave loss in this, one that may some day be made good as cities cease to be the impersonal caravansaries they now are and develop groupings in which the communal play-spirit may again be in evidence.

There is a higher degree of self-fulfillment where the individual has engaged in a planned activity that has taken him into the regions of great human triumphs. For example, he may have carried out over a number of years a study of some science; or have trained himself in the appreciation or the execution of some art; or have made himself master of some period of history; or have participated in some major movement of human amelioration. In all such cases, through organized pursuit of an aim of real moment, the leisure activity has had the chance to grow into a significant scheme of life that has run parallel to the work-life.

A still higher level of self-fulfillment, however, has existed where the line between leisure activity and work activity has altogether disappeared, where the work, in short, has been so entirely identical with the interests and powers of the individual that it has constituted his most essential life. This, no doubt, is the condition nearest to our desire, where work is play and play is work. In such a condition, the self is not two streams of separate interest—or three or four or five, as the case may be—but one stream flowing with unity of power and gathering to itself all the tributaries of interest that the encounters of life offer. For such an individual there is no problem of leisure, for leisure is lifted up into a life creatively integrated; and there is no problem of work, for work is a beloved activity for which even a long life is all too short.

But the life of leisure-in-work and work-in-leisure may attain a level even higher than this. An individual may work in solitude and be happy and effective in his work. But he may be even happier and more effective as he shares in a challenging friendship or love with one whose interests are akin to his own. Or he may carry on his interests in the stimulating atmosphere of a group of co-workers, gaining thereby a diversity of point of view and a continuousness of criticism and encouragement that make his life a rich experience of creative sharing. In such a type of life leisure and work are lifted up into that community of interests which is perhaps the most essential condition of happiness and growth.

THE NEED OF A NEW ATTITUDE

Leisure becomes a civilizing factor as it exhibits the qualities of self-fulfillment rather than escape. Hitherto, we have permitted the leisure life of individuals to shift pretty much for itself, or, worse, we have permitted commercial interests to exploit the leisure hungers of individuals for their own gain. As a society, we have, indeed, given serious attention to training young people to the use of the tools necessary for their life. We have also paid some attention to acquainting them with the cultural background of their civilization. But we have made very little effort to train them to a wise and effective use of their childhood leisure or to prepare them for a wise use of such leisure as may come to them in their later life. Thus, for example, there is little in school education that the child is enabled to carry on into adulthood as a leisure time activity. As a child, he reads childish books, plays childish games, and occupies himself in ways that terminate with his young years. His youthful education leaves him with few leisure activities that can be carried on into adulthood. Again, when he enters adulthood, no effort is made to guide him to those ways of leisure that can serve most effectively to enrich his life and keep him mentally and emotionally growing.

Apparently, one of the major enterprises of a new society must be to take careful stock of leisure as a way of life. There is every reason, for example, why a child should be encouraged not only to the mastery of his lessons, but to the development of those extra-curricular interests in which he builds an eager life for himself. Indeed a well-organized educational system will not consider these to be extra-curricular at all, but as much part of the true education of the child as the learning of multiplication tables, reading, and writing. It is noteworthy that schools of the newer type are moving along these lines, though often against the protest of parents who conceive the leisure life as something that has no part in education. One can easily visualize schools of the future in which every opportunity is given—in workshop, laboratory, art and music studio, in garden, and in excursions in field and forest—for the development in the child of a wider range of interests than has traditionally been contemplated.

As the schools come to regard the leisure life of major importance, the wisdom of their attitude will permeate the homes, and the leisure activities of children will not be the haphazard and inconsequential affairs that they now so largely are. To help children to organize and carry through their ardent interests is to prepare them to be the kind of adults who will not readily succumb to the made-to-order amusements of a commercial world that invites its customers to lay aside their initiative and brains with the turning of a dial or the settling into a seat at a show.

THE PROBLEM OF THE ADULT

Obviously the greatest contribution a society can offer to effective living will be to make possible as widely as it can the kind of life in which the individual's work is identical with an interest that has wide-reaching scope. Where such identity of interests and work obtains there is no problem of stimulating leisure interests or of guiding the individual into areas of activities that will enrich his life. He easily makes a life for himself, in which, of his own initiative, he utilizes all that he is capable of absorbing of what the world has to offer as contributory to his major enterprise.

There will always be a problem, however, in the case of those whose work is only partly identical with their interests or is something wholly alien to their wishes but forced upon them by the necessity of making a livelihood. In such cases, society has a new obligation: namely, to open to adults opportunities for leisure activity which they themselves are incapable of securing. The banality of adult existence throughout the land arises chiefly from the fact that with the disappearance of active communal life because of our increasing urbanization, the individual usually has no adequate means of finding for himself the opportunity for the enrichment of his leisure time. In New York and other large cities, numberless opportunities are at the command of the average individual. He may engage in a course of study, or learn to paint, or join a folk-dancing group, or hear lectures on his favorite topic. In most other cities and towns of the country, practically none of these opportunities is open. Indeed, in communities without libraries or adult educational facilities, the emptiness of opportunity is something almost too appalling to contemplate. To be sure, in many places, groups of alert individuals make such valiant efforts as they can to capture for themselves some measure of release from the general emptiness, but on the whole, the adult population settles down to the easiest way of the daily newspaper, the radio, the movie, and the card club.

Herein, no doubt, is indicated a chief direction that contemporary society will be called upon to take. Adults are destined to have increasing leisure. If this part of their life is to be other than a kind of killing of time that hangs heavy, there must be offered ready opportunity for entrance into activities that have importance as well as interest.

DIFFICULTIES IN THE WAY

There is a dead weight against which any movement for the enrichment of leisure life will have to exert itself: the dead weight of the escape forms of leisure. People, by and large, are not obviously hungering and thirsting after opportunities to occupy their leisure time. They are fully enough occupied as it is. Anyone who has tried it knows how difficult it is in most communities to arouse an interest in intellectual or artistic pursuits. All the evenings of the week, he finds, are fully occupied—with card and cocktail parties, lodge meetings, movies, motor-junketings, listening to the radio—and there is simply no time left for anything else. In short, life in our communities is, paradoxically, so full that no time is left in which to fill the emptiness.

It is a pity that the escape forms of leisure have been given such a headstart. This is probably due as much as anything to an assumption which has hitherto prevailed: namely, that education belongs solely to the years of childhood and youth. The average adult simply does not conceive of his grown-up life as educationally unfinished. Having been taught to believe that when he graduated he was done with all his intellectual preparation, he entered adult life putting away childish things. This pattern of thought so characterizes our existence that the grown-up thinks last of all of occupying his free time with enterprises of self-education. If he has any free time, his first impulse is to use it in ways that are inconsequential.

No doubt the kind of education given in the schools must bear its share of blame for this attitude, for inasmuch as it has operated on the theory that education is a difficult and somewhat disagreeable process that must be endured, it has aroused no awareness of how exciting and exhilarating the pursuit of mental interests can be.

Nevertheless, despite the dead weight of indifference and inconsequentiality, there begin to be signs of an awakening to the need of a kind of life less stagnant and banal. In many places, minorities organize community forums and lecture series, book clubs, orchestras, singing groups, arts and crafts associations, hiking clubs. Sometimes whole communities swing into the movement, as in the small town of Tulare, California, where the Chamber of Commerce, the businessmen's lunch clubs, the women's clubs, the American Legion, the schools, all unite to sponsor a weekly coming-together for lectures, discussion, recreation, and neighborly fellowship. In Des Moines, Iowa, through the initiative of the school system and with the assistance of the American Association for Adult Education, a successful effort has been made to organize forums throughout the city for the discussion of topics vital to present-day civilization. Thousands have attended these forums, indicating that a response may be expected if timely and interesting opportunities are presented. In Delaware, an adult education department has, in a highly successful way, brought to the adults of the whole state opportunities for enrichment that formerly were closed to them.

Enterprises such as these are increasingly effective in breaking down the accustomed thought that adult life is already sufficient unto itself and in developing a delighted awareness among adults that there are ways of occupying their free hours that are not only significant but highly interesting.

No doubt the time is not far distant in which a new assumption will take shape among us: namely, that inasmuch as the individual is to keep on growing, a center of adult leisure activities is as essential to every community as are now the school and the library. As that assumption increasingly prevails, and as such centers multiply, much of the banality that now characterizes our adult existence will disappear.

THE ESSENTIAL QUALITIES

In summary, it may be said that there are four qualities which an adequate form of leisure activity should possess.

In the first place, it should enlist an energetic exercise of the power of selection. Passive enjoyments may be good as far as they go, but they do not go far enough. They call for no marshalling of the mental energies, no projection of the self into the enjoyable situation. Where, on the other hand, there is this energy of selectiveness, the self enters creatively into the leisure enterprise. Thus there is a striking difference between the individual who listens passively to all that the radio pours out upon the unprotesting air, and the individual who, having developed an interest in certain kinds of music or in certain kinds of addresses, makes his own considered choice of that to which he will listen.

In the second place, it should give one a kinship with materials. The individual who has handled a baseball and tried to throw it across a plate has an acquaintance with materials not vouchsafed to the mere spectator. So, in like manner, an individual who plays an instrument or paints a picture or digs a garden has the kind of kinship that places him, so to speak, on the inside of the experience. Robert Frost has described this understanding relation to materials in his lines about Baptiste, his French-Canadian neighbor. Baptiste had interrupted Frost at his woodcutting to make friendly protest against the poorly made axe-helve he was using, and he had invited him to his house to pick a new helve from Baptiste's prized store of them. Frost went, and he makes this comment upon watching Baptiste work at the insertion of a new handle:

"He liked to have it slender as a whipstock,
Free from the least knot, equal to the strain
Of bending like a sword across the knee.
He showed me that the lines of a good helve
Were native to the grain before the knife
Expressed them, and its curves were no false curves
Put on it from without. And there its strength lay
For the hard work. He chafed its long white body
From end to end with his rough hand shut round it.
He tried it at the eye-hole in the axe-head.
'Hahn, hahn,' he mused, 'don't need much taking down.'
Baptiste knew how to make a short job long
For love of it, and yet not waste time either." [5]

In the third place, adequate leisure activity should be of a nature to widen continually the area of one's interest. One may be sure that Baptiste was no narrow specialist, knowing one thing well with a complete finality. It was far more likely that his interest in axe-helves made him an observer whose range of observation was constantly growing and whose wood-wisdom ripened with the years. This is a test which easily enables us to distinguish between the enjoyment which ends in itself and the enjoyment which becomes a starting point for further adventure.

Finally a leisure activity which is to possess fulfilling

[5] Robert Frost, from *The Axe-Helve*; in *Collected Poems of Robert Frost*; by permission of Henry Holt and Company, publishers.

quality should link up with some great line of human interest—as in science, art, literature, craftsmanship, human amelioration—so that as one pursues it, one may companion with master spirits of the race. There is a pathetic kind of isolation in most lives, an isolation that is surprisingly overcome as the individual finds himself thinking the thoughts and appreciating the problems of individuals who have triumphed in some great human way. All worthwhile leisure, then, should lead one beyond one's own activity into a kind of understanding intercourse with the masters of life.

CONCLUSION

The leisure that is to be developed among us will, as we have said, be born out of a world accustomed to significant work. But as it comes to its fullness it will be more than time left over from labor. It will take to itself something of the quality inevitably to be found in a civilization occupied with constructive endeavor. That quality has at times been overstressed, and all work and no play has made Jack a dull boy. But the true quality found in a work-civilization as over against one of privileged classes is the conviction that the activities of life must bear some relation to the whole human enterprise. Hence the kind of leisure that is likely to be developed as our civilization comes to its own will be less and less one of running away from the realities and more and more one of so enriching existence that the very happiness achieved will enhance one's power to ally oneself with the problems and adventures of the common life.

CHAPTER 15. WHERE MODERN MAN IS TO LIVE

IF there are to be new uses of our freedom and new opportunities for our work-life, there must likewise be a new setting for them. Life cannot flourish in a defeating environment. If our modern existence is to be lived with some degree of effectiveness and pleasure, it must be framed by adequate physical conditions.

The civilization of today is essentially one of the city. "Full forty per cent of our people are in great cities and their suburbs, and these show more than half the total growth of the nation in the last decade. In and about Greater London is not far from twenty-five per cent of the population of the United Kingdom. Half the population of Australia is in a half-dozen metropolitan districts. A bare score of such great conurbations over the world center and feature its life and affairs. . . . Generally speaking, however, the evidences are that modern urbanism is not yet in full stride. Indeed, for the scale of the modern world, we may expect bulging cities for at least a century." [1]

There are many people who decry cities, as monstrous,

[1] W. L. Bailey; *Cities Today and Tomorrow;* in *Society Tomorrow,* pages 157, 158; edited by Baker Brownell. Courtesy of D. Van Nostrand Company, publishers.

unwholesome, injurious to the life of individual and family, and who rather hopelessly hope that these huge aggregations will some day be dissolved and the huddled masses of humanity be returned to the land, whence they once issued, and where, for the good of their health and morals, they have always belonged. No doubt much of this feeling is a kind of sentimentalizing induced by romanticized accounts of rural life, and by that inveterate habit which most of us have of believing that the Golden Age has lain somewhere in the past. But much of it has been inspired by a valid distrust of our city civilization and a dislike for what in it is unlovely and life-defeating.

A realistic viewing of the situation, however, must convince one that the city has come to stay, and that while its present forms may be far from ideal, man will never, if he can help it, return to the relative isolation of the traditional forms of rural life. As long as we do not see this, and continue to cast nostalgic eyes beyond our city streets to the land, we shall fail to take up the modern problem of living at its most essential point. For it is in the city that the most noteworthy pioneering of the future is to be done. Formerly the pioneering edge of a civilization was on the frontiers. Men went forth from their settled communities and with axe in hand cleared new territory for habitation. This pioneering edge no longer exists. Whatever opening into a new kind of life there is must now lie within the confines of regions already occupied. The city itself is now a jungle that must be attacked—with its ugliness of slums, its huddled monstrosities of houses that crowd one another to suffocation, its noise and dirt and sunlessness. Within these jungles lie possibilities open to those who would adventure.

"The wrong of unshapely things is a wrong too great to be told." [2]

In short, for the axe of the pioneer, there must now be substituted the brain and the blue print of the architect and the social engineer.

Cities, obviously, are bad not because they are cities but because they are badly conceived cities. There is no reason in the world why man should not live together with his fellow men—doing his work with them and enjoying his pleasures with them. While there is a certain implication of rugged self-dependence in living alone, it may be questioned whether a civilization of near-hermits is any better than one in which people have learned the art of living together in large numbers with considerateness and courtesy.

FALSE INDIVIDUALISM AGAIN

The nineteenth and twentieth century city has suffered from the same defect from which our entire economic order has suffered. It has had no broad social purpose and has therefore been planless. It has sprung up, house after house, factory after factory, skyscraper after skyscraper, in response to individual wish or initiative. Streets have been laid out as the population grew or as commercial interests saw profit in the undertaking. Schools and public

[2] W. B. Yeats, from *The Lover Tells of the Rose in His Heart;* in *Collected Works,* Volume I. (Shakespeare Head Press, Stratford-on-Avon.)

buildings have been erected largely as the accident of land values or the interests of politicians dictated. Railroad terminals have been established at the most immediately convenient points with little reference to the growth of the community and usually without consideration of the possible coördination of competing lines. Factories have been planted wherever they seemed best to serve the purpose of the owners. Shops have been erected in a kind of haphazard disarray in places that seemed profitable.

Such zoning laws as have been effected have, in most cases, been a kind of afterthought when some too glaring atrocity has stirred us out of our customary urban lethargy. In such cases, with an unwonted vigor, we have declared: "This particular evil shall not be allowed to repeat itself in this particular place." But we seem not to have possessed the social imagination to pass beyond such incidental defenses against urban evils.

The result has been something so far from beautiful and so far from effective that one regards the modern city with a kind of amazement at the ugliness and inefficiency to which man's lack of foresight and impetuous individualism have led him.

NEW TRENDS

However, we are gradually awakening to the need for taking our cities in hand. The need has been forced upon us first of all by the inadequacy of present urban facilities for carrying on without inexcusable waste the normal processes of production and distribution. Large cities have been forced to survey their terminal means and lines of transportation—their exits, entrances, and ways of communication. As they have sought to rebuild these more efficiently, wider considerations of urban planning have presented themselves. Allocations of areas for factories and of other areas for distributive enterprises have followed. Park systems have been organized from the point of view of public needs. And finally, the organization of residential quarters has, in a number of cases, gone beyond initial stages of survey into experiments with new types of streets and dwellings.

There has gradually developed a new idea of urban planning, namely, that it must include more than the city proper. It must, as Patrick Geddes, "the Darwin of cities," long ago showed,[3] be regional in scope, including within its area metropolis, suburbs, and countryside. Thus the old conflict between the urban and the rural bids fair to be overcome. The city of tomorrow will doubtless be a planned unit including all types of basic life within its organized regions.

"Stirred by the Great War, London, Paris, and later Berlin, all planned reconstructions on futurist lines. These plans are in action. New York, appalled by the prospect of itself and environs for even so near a future as 1950, has done, perhaps, the most audacious and thorough thinking on the regional city. Chicago, still so largely in the making, and with the prospect of being the world's first mid-continental seaport, is doubtless the most constructively at

[3] See *Cities in Evolution,* and *The Coming Polity, or The Making of the Future.*

work, laying the base-lines, in highways, parks, and zoning control, for a region of a dozen millions of people, in a wide variety of grades and types of community, over some five thousand square miles. Many other regional-city plans are in being. . . .

"The city of tomorrow is in the making on a new basis, on a new scale, and promises realization of the city-idea to a new degree."[4]

THE PRESENT PROBLEM

All of this is significant as we recall the major movements of our recent life. The industrial revolution made us for the most part into a civilization of massed factory workers, shopkeepers and assistants, and urban dwellers. With the coming of the machine, cities grew up like mushrooms, and into the cities poured the countryside. Within these unplanned warrens, men crowded, competed with one another, threw together their more or less characterless structures, shut out air and sunlight, turned their children for their play into the dirty and noisy streets, sought their own pleasures in music hall and pool room.

After a while, as the pressure grew too great for reasonable life to bear, individuals sought breathing spaces outside the crowded metropolis, and the suburbs grew into being. But these, at best, were makeshift places—places of temporary retreat from the ugliness and din of the city. Being little more than sleeping abodes for the

[4] W. L. Bailey; *Cities Today and Tomorrow;* in *Society Tomorrow,* page 184; edited by Baker Brownell. Courtesy of D. Van Nostrand Company, publishers.

male population, they could develop no rounded character of their own. The children who grew up in them could see life only in partial aspect, as a life of shops, nursemaids, and chauffeurs. No genuine community life could be developed. Suburbs, filled every night and emptied every morning of their metropolitan population, were a kind of unhealthy excrescence of the great city.

Meanwhile, outside the suburban area, the countryside was left in more or less stagnant isolation. Scattered villages, without adequate educational or cultural resources, became a kind of primitive hinterland, from which every year, in increasing numbers, the youth went forth to seek the more alluring and lucrative life of the city.

Here, then, is the problem which confronts us today. It is that of making life livable wherever it is lived. City, suburb, and countryside must obviously be transformed if the possibilities of existence that now lie within our control are to be realized. This means that a new conception of the physical organization of our life is necessary. This conception must include life in all its phases and locations. It must involve not only the thinking out anew of how cities should be built, but also how the farthest countryside and the nearer suburban areas should be built. It involves, in short, a conception that is synthetic.

This is regionalism, the planning for whole areas in such a way that all the essential functions are brought into close-knit interrelation. In such regional planning, the farthest rural area is given access to metropolitan opportunities, while the metropolitan dweller is granted the benefits of air, sunshine, and soil that now belong, in adequate measure, only to the rural dweller. For the carrying out of such planning, all the pertinent instrumentalities of our inventive age must be used—highways, parkways, rapid transit, electric lighting and power, a wide-flung educational system, libraries, museums, theatres. The objective is to make the cultural blood really circulate so that there will be neither overconcentrations in urban localities, nor a kind of ambiguous circulation in suburban areas.

MEANS WITHIN OUR POWER

For the execution of such a "planned economy" in regional life, there are devices now at our command. There is first of all the device of zoning, which, in some measure, has already been employed to great advantage in a number of cities. "This type of regulation was scarcely known in the United States in 1916; in 1928, over 30,000,000 live under the control of zoning laws. The movement is still in its infancy and in all probability is destined to a much wider use. Other types of similar regulation, such as parking rules, the exclusion of vehicles of certain types from restricted streets and areas, ordinances regarding the location of bill-boards, and similar 'police' ordinances, will probably be more fully developed, in order to enable citizens more effectually to control their community life and development." [5]

There is, in the second place, the device of new uses of

[5] Ralph E. Heilman; *Modern Industry and Social Control;* in *Society Tomorrow,* page 108; edited by Baker Brownell. Courtesy of D. Van Nostrand Company, publishers.

space. Says Frank Lloyd Wright, in *The Disappearing City,* (page 7; W. F. Payson), "It is already evident that life now must be more naturally conserved by more light, more freedom of movement and a more general spatial freedom in the ideal establishment of what we call civilization. A new space concept is needed. And it is evident . . . that it has come."

Part of this new space concept is the use of the perpendicular. Hitherto we have spread out our cities with house next to house, no one of them reaching more than a few stories high. In the process, we have crowded ourselves to suffocation, so that we move through miles of streets where no space is left between the buildings.

Norman Bel Geddes, in his *Horizons,* gives a suggestive picture of how our cities might recapture the countryside if perpendicularity were put into effective use.[6] "The great value of the tall building in a city is that it towers high, furnishes its inhabitants with more and better air, sunshine, and space than they could possibly get otherwise in an equally populated section. Let us assume that the average height of all the buildings covering one entire block in Lower Manhattan is ten stories. It is considerably less than this. Take fifteen blocks as a unit, each being ten stories in height. Concentrate the floor space of all the buildings in these fifteen blocks into one tower covering one block. Such a tower might be one hundred and fifty stories high.

"Within this one structure, occupying one block, we

[6] *Horizons,* page 285; by permission of Little, Brown, and Company, publishers.

would have the same capacity as all the ten-storey buildings covering the fifteen blocks. As a result fourteen blocks are released for use as open country, or park, or airport, and we have a superior organism as far as an intercommunicating business system is concerned. The business of fifteen blocks is concentrated in one block and intercommunicating by vertical and horizontal transit systems. Multiply this principle by three, and we span the width of Manhattan. The space between each building is greater in width than the width of Central Park. . . .

"The public at large thinks of skyscraper architecture as applying only to large cities. There are many arguments for its application to the small town. All the merchants in a town of five thousand persons will some day pool their interests. Instead of putting up numerous little three-storey and four-storey buildings of their own, they will build *one* tower-type building in the center of the town. This tower will not need to be very high, yet it will make life much easier for the whole community. Mrs. Jones will find it more convenient for her shopping, especially in rainy, hot or cold weather. In rainy weather she will be dry from the time she enters the building until she completes her errands. In hot weather, the building will be cooled by conditioned air, and in cold weather, heated. She will not be going from one draft temperature to another and slipping on icy pavements. The doctor, the movie and the butcher will all be under one roof, along with the commercial and governmental activities of the town, including the theatre and the mayor's office."

These suggestions are sufficient to indicate the uses to

which our architectural and engineering intelligence may be put to redeem life from its present physical uglinesses and inefficiencies. We live in a civilization that grew too rapidly. Like frontiersmen in haste to get to the real business in hand, we clapped together our temporary shelters, and then forgot that they were only makeshifts. Breathing time, however, is at hand. Already we begin to look about us to see how this and that early monstrosity can be removed. Very soon, we shall make broader plans, envisage wider enterprises. The thought will take hold that city, suburb, and countryside are just as much controllable instrumentalities as any other invention of man. When we realize that these instrumentalities may be transformed in ways that will multiply the effectiveness and the satisfactions of our life many times over, we shall mold them more nearly to the pattern of our intelligent interests.

LOCAL GOVERNMENT

There remains, perhaps, our most serious problem—that of urban government. It has been notoriously bad, and many of us are in despair of its ever being better. But here, too, there is a steady movement of our intelligence.

In the first place, we are beginning to recognize the antiquated character of our traditional forms of community government. Mr. Roosevelt has pointed out, in his *Looking Forward*, that we inherit a form of local government dating from the Duke of York's Laws enacted about 1670. Inefficiency has been piled on inefficiency, until we face the curiously baffling situation in which a citizen may live under ten layers of government.

"A citizen so situated has too much governmental machinery to watch. It is too complicated for him to understand. He may not realize that ten sets of officials are appropriating public funds, levying taxes and issuing bonds." [7]

He goes on to describe the waste involved in a vast army of more or less useless officials which this unplanned and poorly organized form of government entails:

"In county and town governments alone in New York State, leaving out incorporated cities and villages altogether, there are about fifteen thousand officials, most of whom are elective and have constitutional status. These include in the counties chiefly county judges, sheriffs, surrogates, county clerks, registrars, district attorneys, coroners, county attorneys, and commissioners of welfare; and in the towns, supervisors, town clerks, justices of the peace, assessors, town collectors, highway superintendents, constables, and welfare officers. These paid officers, with minor exceptions, are found in all counties and towns. They constitute what may be called the regular Army of Occupation. But besides this army of occupation there is an even greater corps of what I would call the Home Guards, paid and unpaid, part and whole time, elective and appointive, representing the police, light, fire, sewer, sidewalk, water, and other local improvement districts and the school dis-

[7] Franklin D. Roosevelt; *Looking Forward,* page 78; by permission of The John Day Company, publishers.

tricts with their boards, superintendents, clerks, and teachers." [8]

The rectification of all this, Mr. Roosevelt contends, lies along the line of a planned consolidation of functions.

It inspires hope to realize that one such form of reorganization has been accomplished. It is that of the council-manager type of government. "The council-manager plan of city government," writes A. R. Hatton, "may fairly be regarded as the greatest American contribution to constructive politics since the framing of the Federal Constitution." [9] It is noteworthy that this new type of city government grew out of the privilege extended to cities to free themselves of state control and work out their own local destinies.

"The city-manager plan, or more properly the council-manager plan, was first introduced in 1908 in a rather defective form. Gradually put into definite legal form and perfected, it won its way by popular adoption into nearly four hundred cities and towns within twenty years after its first appearance. Essentially, there is nothing new in the council-manager idea. In organization it calls for the election of a council of moderate size, and usually from the city at large, in which are placed all the legislative and executive powers of the city government. However, the council is required to have its policies carried out through a chief executive officer appointed by and responsible to

[8] *Ibid.*, page 79.

[9] *The Future of Urban Politics and Government*; in *Society Tomorrow*, page 142; edited by Baker Brownell. Courtesy of D. Van Nostrand Company, publishers.

the council. The chief executive, or manager, is appointed without fixed term, and may be removed by the council at any time. In order that the manager may properly be held responsible by the council, he is usually given full authority to appoint and remove the heads of the various executive departments. . . .

"It is striking testimony to the popularity and effectiveness of council-manager government that within twenty years it should have won its way by popular choice into so many cities and towns. No proposed governmental change has ever been fought more vigorously and viciously by the old political forces. Besides, it has had to overcome in many sincere minds the devotion to the two American political dogmas of elected executives and separation of powers, both of which it discards. The progress of the idea in spite of this opposition still further emphasizes the strong hold which it has taken on the minds of city voters.

"The experience so far had with council-manager government indicates that there are certain results which have so uniformly followed its adoption that even the opponents of the system no longer deny them. These are (1) that the plan has brought into the service of American cities a higher grade of executive ability than they have previously secured, (2) that the financial affairs of council-manager cities are almost invariably better managed than in cities under the old style systems, and (3) that the influence of spoils politics has been greatly reduced and in some places completely eliminated." [10]

Many other experiments no doubt will be made as the

[10] *Ibid.*, page 138 ff.

home rule principle is applied to cities. And as the regional idea of planning swings into effectiveness, it will make possible an escape from our present overlapping of authority and wasteful multiplication of offices.

CONCLUSION

Here, then, as in other matters, we are passing into a new order of existence. The ways of the fathers are no longer ways that fit our modern conditions. As we realize this and use our social intelligence for the planning of our environmental life, there is reason to believe that much of the ugliness and ineffectiveness from which we have long suffered may be made to disappear.

CHAPTER 16. THE EIGHTH ADVENTURE

THE history of the American people might be briefly described as seven adventures in pioneering. The textbooks, for the most part, with their careful concern about dates, battles, treaties, political controversies, and territorial expansions, tend to obscure the grand simplicity of our career. But when we disregard the complexity of historical details and hold ourselves strictly to the more fundamental movements of our life, we gain a sense of major directions.

THE SEVEN ADVENTURES

Our career as a people may be said to have begun in an act of spiritual pioneering. The Pilgrim Fathers left their homeland because they demanded for themselves the right to worship the God in whom they believed in the way in which they believed. Our essential history, in short, began in a protest against spiritual tyranny.

The second stage of our career was marked by a second act of pioneering. We demanded the right to be duly represented in the government of our life. When we were denied the right, we fought for it, and, winning the fight, we established a new form of political government of and for and by its citizens.

The third act of pioneering is not so generally identified. One looks almost in vain, even in the textbooks, for any sufficient recognition of its originality and importance. In this third act, we registered a protest against another kind of tyranny—that of ignorance. We realized that no people could be politically free and at the same time, in large numbers, ignorant. So, against strong forces of opposition among ourselves and in the face of the incredulity of an aristocratically conditioned world, we established education for everyone.

The fourth act of pioneering is still remembered as one of the bitterest periods in our national history. We emancipated the slave. We declared that for all time racial enslavement was not to be tolerated in our midst. And again, because forces that wished to perpetuate a tyranny would not join in what many of us conceived to be just, we took up arms and fought for this new type of justice.

The fifth act of pioneering, like the third, is, in its full significance, not generally recognized. We addressed ourselves to the conquest of the hitherto uncontrolled and unutilized forces of Nature. This, to be sure, was an achievement not exclusively American. The harnessing of Nature's forces through machines for the serving of man's purposes had already begun in England, but the development and organization of technological skills made such rapid strides in America—particularly following the Civil War—that we were soon well in advance of the rest of the world in the enterprise of opening up new material possibilities for the relief and enrichment of life.

There followed the sixth act of pioneering—the conquest of sex-tyranny. Here, again, America has no exclusive claim to honor. Other peoples of the world had already advanced to the conception that women must be regarded in all essentials as equals of men. Nevertheless, despite the leadership of other nations, there were in America age-old forces of male conservatism that required decades of courageous pioneering for their overcoming. In the end, the movement for sex-justice swept the country with an almost incredible rapidity, and the equality of men and women became an established principle in our life.

Finally, there was the seventh act of pioneering. There are many who would not regard it so, but rather as an act of vast self-delusion. But at least it may be said that the rank and file of Americans sincerely believed, during the Great War, that they were called upon to "make the world safe for democracy." In that spirit, they gave their substance and their lives for what they conceived to be a cause of profound and immediate moment. If we now register cynicism at the self-delusion—or better at the propaganda-induced delusion—we must nevertheless recognize in the kind of response given to the call to arms a spirit akin to all the other pioneerings—in brief, a wish to oppose tyranny and a desire to make the world genuinely free for the habitation of free individuals.

THE SEVEN DEFEATS

Seven acts of pioneering. In them, it may be said, lies the essential history of America. But now a disappointing aspect of this history becomes apparent. Each of these enterprises was one of which a nation might justly be proud; but like many another enterprise undertaken in a spirit of courage and good faith, each of them failed to carry itself to completion. Thus no sooner did the Pilgrim Fathers plant their freedom-seeking feet upon this continent, than they proceeded to institute a spiritual tyranny of their own. It is not necessary here to recall in detail the cruel intolerance they exhibited toward those whose belief differed from theirs. Persecution and banishment were the reward of any who presumed to claim the right to freedom of worship.

Thus our first American venture in freedom turned into a kind of defeat, one that still meets us throughout the land—in the bitter and ofttimes violent attempts of believers of one faith to coerce others into their way of thinking or to prevent the free expression of beliefs other than their own. One need merely recall the anti-evolution activities in the southern states, the anti-Catholic activities of some of our widespread organizations, the notable fact that a Catholic nominee for president was campaigned against on the ground of his religion, and the still more notable fact that disbelief in a monotheistic god is in many cases a disqualification for office.

America, in short, beginning its career in a demand for

practice old sex disabilities rest upon women almost as heavily as ever.

We have already intimated the failure of the seventh adventure. Conceived in an ardor of idealism, the effort, by force of arms, to make the world safe for democracy has resulted in new, bewildering tyrannies. Even within our own land, most of the privileges of a free people have, in one way or another, been abrogated—particularly, in many places, those of free speech and assembly; unprecedented acts of ruthlessness upon dissenting minorities have been perpetrated; our most "patriotic" societies have developed the art of blacklisting their fellow citizens; a vast money power has grown into an almost complete control of our life; while new tyrannies of racketeering have held unofficial sway over our legitimate enterprises.

THE NEW ADVENTURE

There is, indeed, a grand simplicity about our American history. It is the simplicity of repeated efforts to achieve, in one way or another, a release of life from its various tyrannies. But there has likewise been this curious inability to carry efforts through to triumph.

At the present time we are obviously on the threshold of a new adventure. Is it to be simply another one, doomed, like the rest, to a large measure of failure? Or is there the possibility that through the next enterprise of pioneering we may bring the older adventures of our American life more nearly to their completion?

It would indeed invest our past with a new kind of

vitality if the present could be regarded as a period in which old undertakings were to be undertaken anew, in which enterprises begun by our forefathers were to be given a better chance of fulfillment. Our tendency, too largely, is to regard the past as finished. But perhaps the best reverence we can offer to the past is to take up the work the fathers began and carry it forward in ways and to an extent impossible in their day.

The possibility of so doing seems not altogether remote, for the new adventure that appears to be ahead of us involves elements that bear fundamentally upon all our past endeavors. If one can judge by the kind of thinking that seems to be taking shape, this new adventure is heading for a reconstructed view of life. Characteristic attitudes are emerging into expression: the attitude, for example, of regarding the common welfare as paramount; the attitude of assuring to all the right of a secure and wholesome life; the attitude of removing the instrumentalities of force and national aggressiveness; the realization that a new era of leisure is ahead and that the agencies of social life must be directed toward a greater enrichment of its citizenry; the attitude of breaking down walls—of nationality, race, and religion—and achieving more nearly than hitherto a unification of man on this planet.

"Mankind," writes Dr. Whitehead in his *Adventures of Ideas*, "is now in one of its rare moods of shifting its outlook." Special outlooks have shifted in our American past. The present shifting of outlook would seem to involve something far more fundamental and comprehensive. It would seem, in effect, to involve a basically new philosophy of life. It is one that goes beyond the sophistication of self-interest, of each for himself. It goes even beyond the genial casualness of "live and let live." It would seem to be more adequately expressed in the phrase: "Live and help live." For the new outlook would seem already to be presupposing a common interest in the welfare of every member of society.

The present issue, to be sure, takes chiefly the guise of economic and political problems. But the manner of meeting these problems is essentially more than economic and political. It involves a reconstructed view of human values. We have, in brief, reached a point in our civilization where the inadequacies of older attitudes and practices come sharply into relief. Thus the intolerances of religious absolutism and sectarianism seem increasingly out of place in an age that has learned both the tentativeness and the unlimited extent of scientific inquiry; thus, also, the localisms of nations seem curiously out of date in an age that knows both the delight and the liberation of moving swiftly, in transportation and communication, over the face of the globe; thus the tragedy of poverty seems without excuse in a time when the triumphs of science and invention have, for the first time in history, made universal abundance possible.

Racial intolerance will, no doubt, be long in the overcoming, but it is significant that today any too obvious indications of concerted racial oppression are met by widespread protests. Doubtless these protests are not yet widespread enough to indicate that contemporary man transcends in his feeling the boundaries of race. There will be required many decades of swift movement over the face of the earth and much crossing of all kinds of frontiers before that condition is reached. But in the very effort to achieve a more acceptable economic and political status in modern life, there is developing a growing sensitiveness to human values which will, in the long run, tend to wear away the hardness of our racial prejudices.

In this growing sensitiveness to human values, the place of women in the scheme of things will no doubt be more generously conceived. The simple attempt to make women equals of men was apparently too simple. It overlooked too many real distinctions. No doubt, what is already developing among us is a deepening sense of the unique part that women can play in a more humane organization of our life. As they begin to play that part, they will be admitted not as tolerated subordinates in a man's world, but as complementary participators in the enterprise of carrying life to more acceptable levels.

THE PARAMOUNT REVOLUTION

What is happening among us today is what, in older terminology, might be called a quickening of the soul of man. Unfortunately I do not know the source of the following, written by Vernon Lee, but I am venturing to use it because of its expression of a significant point of view. It deals with an economic question; but instantly we perceive that the spirit which pervades the writing is far more than economic:

"Art, music, beautiful nature, poetry, and that queer

chaos within our souls of fragmentary and mingled impressions whence all things beautiful arise, into which all things beautiful resolve—all this has in reality but one fault: that it is unequally distributed. The pity of it is that we, a small class, monopolise all of such consoling things. . . . The cause of dissatisfaction in many minds, and of a degree even of hostility towards the beautiful uselessnesses of the world, is moreover that these same beautiful uselessnesses which ought in justice to be possessed by all, so often serve to withdraw the attention of those who do possess them . . . from the necessities of the very creatures who possess in this world nothing save the miserable slightness of their own wants, and who among other birthrights of mankind, are disinherited also of beauty. . . .

"Similarly with beautiful things. There is no doubt that we, privileged people, are given too much of them and give them too much of our attention; but that is not saying that in the world at large there is too much of them or too much attention given thereunto. . . . One result, let us hope, of our thinking somewhat of matters less pleasant, may be, in the long run, in the long-expected future, which yet sometimes comes with a rush, that the less selfish work of the world will be no longer the mere removal of evil, but also the distribution of good; and among the various sorts of good, one of the best is beauty."

There is a kind of plea for pity in that, and for justice. It is the plea of a spirit wounded by the indifferences and cruelties which attend our ordinary behaviors. Why must we have this bitter-ugly world of dispossessing, of passionate acquisitiveness, when the beautiful uselessnesses might be as free and as accessible as the air we breathe under clean heavens?

It is this plea which is the growing note of spiritual revolt in our world. Our ways of life, we realize, have been too low for such greatness of life as lies within us. It is this spiritual revolt which underlies all others, and it is in the pursuance of this demand that life be made adequate to its possibilities that this new adventure becomes more important and more profoundly revolutionary than all the others. As it moves toward its completion, it must fulfill what the other enterprises were unable to accomplish for the reason that no one of them was sufficiently thorough-going in its demands. The Pilgrim Fathers had a sense of spiritual freedom—for themselves. They could not sense a generous freedom for all. Our political forefathers could conceive of a democracy of the ballot; they could not yet conceive of that equality of life-opportunity without which the equality of the ballot becomes a farce. The founders of our schools could conceive of a battle against illiteracy; they could not yet conceive of that more significant and enduring battle which confronts ignorance and prejudice in all their forms and which should make the school—from our infancy to old age—the place of a seeking unhampered and unafraid. The emancipators of the slave could visualize one kind of slavery; they were as yet too restricted in vision to realize the thousand-fold forms of bondage that must be removed before man—black or white—could be called truly free.

The makers of machines could conceive of conquering nature; they were too shortsighted to realize that there were forces in man himself that needed conquering if the very machine was not to become a monstrosity and a despair. The emancipators of women could visualize the removal of a single disability; they could not yet see that this disability was but one of many, and that only by a profoundly reconstructed view of the place of both men and women in society could women be truly liberated. The fighters for a world made safe for democracy could visualize the defeat of an immediate enemy; their own efforts at peace, following the war, indicated all too clearly that they did not realize—among themselves and their foes—a far more wide-flung enemy that needed overcoming.

Today there is the plea among us for a more than verbal justice, the plea for a new viewing of the possibilities of life. But what is even more significant, it is a plea that begins to be made throughout the world. The spiritual revolution in our American thought and institutions is being duplicated among civilized peoples everywhere. As it gains in momentum, it is due to carry to some measure of completion the older enterprises of emancipation.

"Humanity," wrote Jan Smuts some years ago, "has struck its tents, and is again on the move." It is civilization that is moving, an old civilization advancing into a new one. It is the individualistic state changing into the social state. There may, indeed, be ahead of us a requisite forty years of wandering in the wilderness, but there are unmistakable pillars of cloud by day and of fire by night that encourage us in the belief that we are in fact moving toward our own promised land.

INDEX

INDEX